Center Path Relationships

A Study of the Governing Principles

True Principles Series

Book One

By Gary Moe

Visit us at www.TruePrinciples.com

ISBN 978-1-7923-2179-5

Printed in USA

Table of Contents

Introduction

I was working with an executive of a high tech company a few years ago. He was having some challenges with other members of the executive team. I sat down with him and we walked through the governing principles of relationships and how they work. As we were about to start our third meeting, he said, "Gary, everything you are describing makes perfect sense to me, but I have to admit that I was skeptical about applying the principles, that you were suggesting, in my professional relationships. Instead, I went home and tried them with my son." He paused, looked me straight in the eye as if searching for something, and then continued, "I am currently enjoying the best relationship I have ever had with my son. Ever! And it only took two days." He paused again and then said, "I was wondering if you would be willing to come to my house, start over again, and teach my wife and I these principles and how to use them. I need to hear it again and she needs to hear it with me. We both need this." I was happy to, and we had a very enjoyable time.

I find that most people who wish for better relationships are trying hard to make improvements and usually they are close, but the one or two key elements they need are just slightly beyond what they can see. The principles that govern relationships describe the fundamental elements of all relationships. It does not matter if the relationship is the product of family, work, or a social life. The principles are easy to understand, and they are universally applicable.

In another instance, I was working with an entire executive team. They were struggling with the relationships they had with each other. After the first workshop, the CEO let me know that he was going to invite his wife to participate. About a week later, the CEO pulled me aside and said, "My wife and I have a new pass-time. We go to the mall, find a comfortable place to sit, and then we watch other people. We can pick out those who are using the relationship principles correctly and those who are not, exactly as you described. Gary, I have to tell you. The principles you are teaching us are not rocket science by any stretch, but they are profound. I never would have seen them if you had not pointed them out, but now that you have, I can see them as clear as day."

This book is not a book of anecdotes describing what to do in a given situation for a certain type of relationship. That is way too complex and too difficult to manage. Instead, I discuss the principles that govern all relationships and describe how to apply them every time, everywhere, with everyone. Being universally applicable is what makes a principle. Any approach less than the application of a principle does not have the power to make a sustainable improvement.

A few years ago, a person told me about a relationship she was in that she described as being "toxic." She had heard about the principles and wanted to know a little more. We walked through them, but she was had doubts saying that she had been in this "toxic" relationship for years was not sure that there was any hope of it ever changing, but she was willing to give the principles a try.

From that moment and for years since, she has her own unique way of greeting me. When we see each other, she will walk up to me, smile, and say, "Life changing." The principles had such a profound effect on the relationship that an outside observer would not even recognize it from years ago.

There are many things that are important in life, but none so important that they overshadow relationships. Compared to all other potential sources, only productive relationships can produce long-term, sustainable happiness. Other sources can produce bursts of happiness. They can be very rewarding in the moment and for some period of time afterward, but they fall short of being sustainable and producing feelings of long-term fulfillment. The potential is so great and the rewards so abundant that it is worth whatever investment is necessary to obtain and reside within productive relationships. This book will show you how to be effective in your efforts.

Prologue

Forty years ago, I spent some time in the beautiful country of Ecuador. One hot summer morning, I was walking on a cobble stone road in the small town of Playas when I heard someone in the distance calling my name. I turned to see an elderly lady, not quite 4 feet tall, shuffling her way toward me, stopping every few steps to wave her cane in my direction. I had met her briefly about a week before, so I was surprised that she would remember my name and even more surprised that she was out trying to find me. I walked toward her, and she continued to call my name until she was almost to me where she stopped to catch her breath. After a moment she said, "I have been looking for you all morning. We Ecuadorians are accustomed to the sun, but your gringo skin will burn so I brought you a hat." She had been out all morning wandering the streets of town looking for me so that she could give me a hat. I was in awe that she would be this thoughtful and would do something so kind — for me – a virtual stranger.

Forty years later, I still have that hat and the lessons about relationships which she taught me that morning and in dozens of other encounters I had with her over the next few months. I have learned many things from many people through my life. When it came time for me to learn about humility and selflessness, she was one of my most valued teachers.

CHAPTER I

I wonder…

The experiences we have in relationships can be some of the most beautiful, rewarding, and memorable events of our lives. Productive relationships bring balance to our perspectives, serve as a check on self-indulgence, allow us to do more, and inspire us to be better.

Unfortunately, I have also seen the other side of relationships. I have both observed and participated in relationships that were not as productive as they could have been, were struggling, or became so strained they did not survive.

Over the years, this wide spectrum of experiences and observations have led me to ask myself:

What causes some relationships to be productive and successful and others to become unproductive and strained? When I do something by myself, outside of a relationship, I determine my own success, but with relationships, it seems that I can influence only half of the success because I am relying on the other person for the rest. What if I want the relationship to be successful, but the other person is unwilling to work as hard as I am or does not want success as much as I do? Some people consider ending such relationships, but what if it is one you cannot or should not end such as with a family member, a co-worker, a customer, or a neighbor? I cannot walk away from those. Am I just stuck? Is my hope to simply endure it? Is there a way I can influence greater success if I want it to be successful?

My thoughts continued:

I get to choose my spouse and my friends. Circumstance chooses all the rest of my relationships for me. If circumstance is choosing all these people without my say, is it possible to have successful relationships with all of them or is that expectation simply too great? In a strained relationship, I would often feel that I could not influence even half of the success. Should my expectation be, instead, that a successful relationship is a matter of random and unpredictable luck? Is it a matter of statistical percentages or happening upon the right person?

I have met people who believe that success is purely luck. They depend on luck to carry them through the day because their experience tells them that relationships are too unpredictable. They enjoy the occasional *good time* and endure the rest.

I have a hard time accepting that I am reliant upon luck or percentages for my success. I have relationships with too many people who are important to me to leave success up to chance.

If encountering the right person is the determining factor, then marriages and friendships would be the stellar examples of productive relationships. Unfortunately, high divorce rates indicate otherwise plus this still does not account for those people, even though they were chosen by circumstance, who are important to me. I need and want to have a good relationship with all of them independent of whether they meet the criteria of the "right person", whatever that happens to be.

I am most settled in life when I can see things clearly. Participating in a strained relationship was anything but clear to me. In fact, many days I would find myself feeling like it was a complete mystery. I could not understand how I could be in such a situation and be at such a loss of knowing what to do. I did what I thought I was supposed to do. I did what people suggested I should do, but nothing helped. After it fell apart, I retreated, regrouped, and then returned to my original question: *What causes some relationships to be productive (meaning rewarding, fulfilling, uplifting, satisfying, etc.) and others to become so unproductive (draining, stifling, heavy, etc.) and strained?*

I decided to do whatever was required to answer my question.

I have one quality that I know I am good at. I am good at taking a question or a problem, studying it, and coming up with a way to see it from a perspective that helps me solve it. I believed that this would have to be my approach. I did not believe I would find the answer in some hidden solution that no one had yet discovered. Instead, I believed that I was missing something in the way I saw and understood relationships. I needed to see things with a different perspective — a perspective that would be new for me and maybe it would be new for others as well.

After considerable time, effort, observation, and contemplation, I finally discovered that new perspective that I believed was there. It answered my question. In fact, it has answered all my questions on relationships thus far. The thing I find fascinating is that it continues to answer my questions as new ones arise.

In the process of trying to find this new perspective, I went back to the mountain of suggestions, recommendations, and anecdotes to be or to do so many things thinking that maybe I missed something there. Now, in the light of this new perspective, I can see that all those suggestions and recommendations are good and have a role to play in a relationship, but they are incomplete. Many of them address the symptoms of a strained relationship, but not the cause of the strain. Some actually can address the cause of the strain, but not by themselves or, more ironically, not in the way they were suggested. I even found a number of suggestions that, by all indications, appear to be the right things to do. However, when seen more clearly they turn out to be entirely the wrong things to do. They cause strain instead of relieving it.

Even after discovering this new perspective, I have spent the last fifteen years testing it with every kind of situation and circumstance I can throw at it to see if there is any aspect of the perspective that is faulty or incomplete. The amazing outcome of all these tests is that the perspective has never stopped teaching me. It has taught me some amazing things about the elegant purpose and design of relationships.

I finally feel confident enough that I have tested it enough and have learned enough that I can share it more broadly. My hope in sharing this perspective is that it will help you as much as it has helped me. Even if it helps you only a fraction of how much it has helped me, it will be worth it to you.

The purpose of this book is to show you relationships from a different perspective. I hope to help you see with new eyes so that you can enjoy better relationships by improving the good ones or repairing those that are currently strained or in poor condition.

CHAPTER II

Seeing a New Perspective

Seeing a new perspective requires that we look at familiar things in a different way. We need to fight tendencies of continuing with conclusions we have already drawn. Instead, we need to build our perspective from the ground up.

Let's start with defining a couple of things and then we will start building the landscape of the new perspective.

Relationship: A relationship exists between two people. A person may refer to a relationship with a group of people such as a family or a company, but the reference is only figurative. A relationship with a group is really a reference to the sum of the relationships that person has with individuals in the group.

A relationship begins when two people start interacting and it will continue as long as they continue interacting.

Relationship Partners: These are the two people engaged in a relationship. They are partners in the interactions they have with each other.

The Landscape

The first thing we need is to understand why relationships exist. What is their purpose?

We spend most of our time every day of our lives meeting the demands of reality. Having a job, making a living, paying bills, cooking, eating, sleeping, working out, resting, getting up in the morning, getting dressed, fixing things, doing laundry, shopping, getting an education, solving a problem, and so forth are all examples of meeting the demands of reality. Driving somewhere is composed of a string of demands that we have to meet in order to successfully arrive at our desired destination. Virtually every activity we engage in is a response to a demand from reality.

The purpose of a relationship is to help the partners in the relationship meet demands. Some demands are much easier to meet when two people are involved. Some demands require the second person because they cannot be met by the first person or they cannot be met by only one person. Some demands are just nicer or more enjoyable to meet inside a relationship rather than outside of one.

Meeting demands is going to be an important component of the new perspective.

Before I started this project, relationships seemed complex. When I began looking at them in depth, I found even more complexity. There is such a variety of relationships such as family, work, friends, social situations, etc. There are the unique qualities each person brings to their relationships and there are so many variables, situations, and circumstances that come into play.

To be manageable, this complexity has to be boiled down into fundamental elements that are common to all relationships independent of type, duration, circumstance, current state of productivity, and so forth.

I discovered that there are fundamental elements common to all relationships. As I was trying to understand these fundamental elements and how they worked, I made a discovery that changed everything I thought I knew about relationships. I discovered that these fundamental elements, common to all relationships, are governed by principles. That means they behave the same way every time, everywhere, for everyone.

A principle is a basic truth that, when applied correctly, can produce a predictable and repeatable outcome.

It is important that we understand each part of this definition.

Basic: A fundamental or foundational element.

Truth: Things as they really are. Truth describes the nature of a thing and how it behaves. If something is true, then it is trustworthy, dependable, predictable, and repeatable. For something to be true, it must pass the test of working every time, everywhere, for everyone.

Truth can be described as a principle. For example, the natural laws that govern flight are often referred to as the Principles of Flight.

When applied correctly: When a principle is applied correctly, it will produce a positive result that is dependable, predictable, and repeatable. In other words, correct application of a principle will give the same result every time, everywhere, for everyone. Inversely, there are boundaries of correct application. Trying to function outside the defined boundaries will produce an unproductive or negative result that, too, is dependable, predictable, and repeatable. This implies if I want a positive result, all I need to do is correctly apply the associated principle. It also implies if I am getting a negative result, then it is because I did not apply the principle correctly. Instead, I violated some aspect of the principle or tried to operate outside its prescribed boundaries.

Can produce a predictable and repeatable outcome: A principle describes how something behaves. Correct application of the principle allows a person access to the benefit the principle produces. If I want to produce a given outcome, then I need to know the principle that governs that outcome and I need to know how to apply it. The outcome is predictable and repeatable because it is described by a true principle.

What impact does this have on relationships? It means that there are a set of basic truths that govern how all relationships behave and function. When a person knows these truths and applies them correctly, they can improve their relationships.

The implication goes even further. I have discovered that the principles governing relationships are powerful enough that, if applied correctly by only one of the relationship partners, they will have a positive impact on the entire relationship. I have also discovered that this can happen even if the other relationship partner is initially unaware or even unwilling to apply the principle(s) himself or herself.

So far, we have discovered that the landscape of this new perspective is composed of the following components:

1) The purpose of relationships is to meet demands.
2) The complexities of relationships can be boiled down to fundamental elements common to all relationships.

3) These fundamental elements are governed by principles.
4) This means that principles govern relationships.

As a person becomes aware of the Principles of Relationships and applies them correctly and consistently, he or she can proactively guide improvements in his or her relationships.

Know for Yourself

I realize that these are bold statements and that they may be received with some skepticism.

The beauty of principles, being basic truths, is that they work every time, everywhere, for everyone. You do not have to accept my word on the matter. Simply apply the principles for yourself and see what happens. You can know, from your own experience, if they work or not — if they are true or not.

As we go through the principles, I will invite you to apply them and experience for yourself the impact they have on your relationships.

A few years ago, I had the opportunity to share these principles with an executive in a corporation. He was faced with some challenges at work and was looking for possible solutions. He was skeptical about trying the principles at work, so he went home and applied them with his teenage son to see what would happen. He came to me two days later and explained his experiment and then said, "I am currently enjoying the best relationship I have ever had with my son and it only took two days." He was genuinely surprised at how fast it had occurred and how much progress he and his son had made. This is just one example of how powerful these principles are in bringing about improvement.

Notes

CHAPTER III

The Principles of Relationships

You probably have a relationship you would like to improve. If so, I expect you are looking for help and for something you can do right now. I have organized this book in a way that will give you a powerful tool and an explanation of how to use it by the end of *Chapter 5*.

Let's get you ready to use that tool.

Principles of Relationships

There are four principles that govern relationships. They are the **Principle of Choice**, the **Principle of Interactions**, the **Principle of Relationship Maturity**, and the **Principle of Unity**.

Each principle has one or more laws associated with it. I will introduce a principle with its accompanying laws and describe each of them.

Principle of Choice

The first Principle of Relationships is the **Principle of Choice.** It has only one law which is: *Both relationship partners have the freedom to choose.*

Correct application of this principle requires that I retain my freedom to choose and protect the same for my partner. If either relationship partner tries to stifle or take away the other's choice, then the principle has been violated and the relationship will be negatively impacted.

For some people, this principle is problematic because it gets in the way of a person's idea of how relationships function. For example, a person may think, "If I cannot get you to do what I want, then how are we going to have a good relationship?" Taking this a step further, one of the most frequent problems that comes up in a relationship is conflicting wants. "I want one thing and you want another, now what? If I could just get you to stop choosing to want the things you want, then life would be so much easier for me and our relationship." Have you ever observed that?

It may seem that we are at a crossroad of either applying the principle or having a good relationship, but not both. I will show you how it is possible to apply the principle and have a good relationship, but first we need to talk about another principle.

Principle of Interactions

The second principle is the **Principle of Interactions**. This principle is composed of four laws. You need to understand the first two laws now so you can use the relationship improvement tool I told you about. We will explore the other two later. The first two laws are:

> I. *Interactions are the building blocks of all relationships.*
> II. *An interaction is composed of five events. These events transpire the same way every time, everywhere, for everyone.*

Let's look at each law in more detail.

> I. *Interactions are the building block of all relationships.*

The following points explain why interactions are the building blocks of relationships.

- A relationship exists whenever two people interact. The relationship comes into existence at the first interaction and will endure for as long as the two people continue to interact. A relationship could be as short as a single interaction, it could last a lifetime as in familial and spousal relationships, or it could last for any length of time in between.

- The quality of the relationship is determined by the quality of the interactions.

     When I ask someone, "How is your relationship?" they will give me a subjective response like, "It's good," or "It's OK," or "It's not so great," or "It's strained," etc. They come up with this subjective assessment by evaluating the outcomes, positive or negative, of recently transpired interactions. For example, let's say that we observe fifty-seven productive interactions and four unproductive interactions between two people over the course of a week. Their interaction outcomes are the basis for their assessment of their relationship. One partner might conclude that the relationship is great and improving because of the ratio of fifty-seven to four is positive in his or her mind. The other partner might conclude that the relationship is in trouble because they did have four unproductive interactions or because one of the four was really bad. Neither conclusion is right or wrong, they are simply individual assessments.

     The point is that they are judging the quality of the relationship based on an assessment of interaction outcomes.

- If a person can influence a more positive outcome in the interactions he has with his partner, then the relationship will naturally improve.

This last point is fundamental to the new perspective I am sharing with you. If I am in a relationship that needs improving, what do I do? What am I supposed to focus on? This last point tells me that if I want to improve my relationship, I have to improve the quality of the interactions I am having in that relationship.

So, how do I do that? The next law begins to answer this question. As we look at this law, I would like for you to recall two of the components we have discussed as being part of this new perspective. They are: 1) The purpose of relationships is to help the partners meet demands, and 2) There are fundamental elements common to all relationships.

II. *An interaction is composed of five events. These events transpire the same way every time, everywhere, for everyone.*

When one of the relationship partners faces a demand and wants help in meeting it, he or she will initiate an interaction and invite participation from the other person. The interaction begins with his or her presentation of a *want* to the other partner.

This second law explains that an interaction always takes place in five events. These five events of an interaction are some of the common elements found in all relationships. If I can learn how to successfully step through these five events, then my interactions will be more successful which will cause my relationship to be more successful.

I have labeled these five interaction events as:

1) Partner
2) Choose
3) Learn
4) Contribute
5) Check

I will briefly introduce each event here and then we will explore them in more detail later.

Event 1. Partner: Prior to actually interacting, the partners will determine how they want to interact with each other. The initiating partner will do it prior to presenting the *want*. The responding partner will do it right after the *want* has been presented.

Event 2. Choose: The initiating partner presents a *want* and invites participation. The responding partner considers the *want* and decides if he or she is willing to participate in addressing it.

Event 3. Learn: The third event focuses on formulating a response to the *want*. The formulating process is a learning process in that it involves gathering and assembling facts about the *want* and how to address it.

Event 4. Contribute: The responding partner delivers his or her response.

Event 5. Check: Both partners check the results of the interaction.

As I said, I will explain each of these events in more detail later. I simply wanted you to know they exist at this point.

The thing I want you to be aware of right now is the fact that the relationship partners make contributions during the interaction. These contributions take place when initiating partner presents a want and invites participation and when the responding partner contributes a response to the want.

Throughout this book, I will invite you to do some homework assignments. Please consider doing them. If we were meeting in person, we would do the exercises together so you could have the experience. Since we are not meeting in person, doing the exercises will give you the experience you need with this new perspective so it will become easier to see.

Homework assignment:

1) Observe other people having interactions. See if you can start identifying the presentation of the want and the contribution in response.
2) Even though you are observing, see if you can detect the results the two partners are experiencing from their interactions.

3) After observing for a while, see if you can detect the presentation of the want and the responding contribution in your own interactions.

4) Keep a journal. Record some examples of what you observe and any insights you gained from your observations.

Notes

CHAPTER IV

Relationship Fabric

So far, I have shared the following perspectives about relationships with you:

1) The purpose of relationships is so that partners can help each other meet demands.
2) There are common elements found in all relationships. These elements are governed by principles which means that relationships are governed by principles.
3) Interactions are the building blocks of relationships. I can improve the quality of my relationship by improving the quality of my interactions.

Now I am going to share a key insight of the new perspective.

One of the most common reasons relationships struggle is because they are not strong enough to support the weight of the demands that the partners or reality place on them.

The best way I can describe this is to use an analogy that I am going to call *relationship fabric*.

If you look closely at fabric, you will see that it is composed of many thin threads all woven together. The individual threads are not very strong by themselves but woven together they make fabric that is flexible and durable.

Now imagine that an interaction between two people is like passing a strand of thread between them. Each time they interact, they introduce another strand of thread that gets woven to the others. Over time, the interactions have created a fabric shared between the partners.

This shared fabric represents their capacity to respond to demands that are brought to the partnership. Early in a relationship, the fabric will consist of only a few strands. The relationship is only able to support small and very light demands. As the fabric becomes thicker and more durable, the partners can support heavier demands.

Now let me go back to the key insight I just introduced: *One of the most common reasons relationships struggle is because they are not strong enough to support the weight of the demands that the partners or reality place on it.*

The demands being brought to the relationship are too heavy to be supported by the relationship. The demands tear holes in the relationship and fall to the ground un-met.

The reason this happens is because the partners do not know how to determine relationship strength and they do not understand how to measure the weight of a demand.

This is what I am going to show you next. This is the tool I told you I would help you prepare to use. You will be able to use it as soon as you know how it works.

My objective is to show you how to measure relationship strength, how to measure demand weight, and how to match the two.

We are going to look at relationship strength by using *relationship maturity* as the unit of measure.

It's now time to introduce the **Principle of Relationship Maturity**. It is composed of six laws. The first three laws are:

 I. *Relationship maturity is observable and can be measured by the level of contribution both partners are willing to make.*

 II. *There are seven levels of maturity that a relationship may achieve. Each level is characterized by a type of contribution.*

Let's look at each law in more detail.

I. Relationship maturity is observable and can be measured by the level of contribution both partners are willing to make.

Relationship Maturity refers to the state of the relationship, not that of the individual relationship partners. The maturity of the partners and the maturity of the relationship function independent of each other. Having one does not mean that you necessarily have the other. Mature partners may easily be engaged in an immature relationship and immature partners can be participants in a mature relationship.

The maturity of a relationship is observable and measurable. Maturity is measured by levels of interaction contributions.

Both partners bring contributions to an interaction as they participate in it. These contributions made in the interaction can be observed and measured. I will explain more about how this is done with the second law.

II. There are seven levels of maturity a relationship may achieve. Each level has a maturity requirement and is characterized by the contributions willingly made by the participants.

I have diagramed these levels of maturity in a model called the **Relationship Maturity Model™**.

The **Relationship Maturity Model™** is the first tool you need when you set out to improve a relationship. I am first going to explain what it is, and then I will explain how it works and how it will help you.

Let's look at each relationship maturity level, the maturity requirement associated with that level, and the contribution both partners need to make for their relationship to function at that level.

Level 1

The maturity requirement of level 1 is *acceptance*. This requirement means that the two partners acknowledge the fact that the other person exists and occupies space. The contribution that they make to each other is that they will not try to occupy that same space while the other is there. That is the full extent of the requirement.

This is the least mature level in any relationship. However, I need to point out that a low level of maturity is not necessarily a bad thing. This level of relationship maturity is completely adequate and appropriate for motorists, pedestrians, riders on mass transit systems, people standing in line, etc. This is the fundamental level of interaction we have with the general public.

Example: Let's say that I am walking down the sidewalk and I see you coming towards me. In just a few seconds we are going to pass. We are engaged in a level 1 relationship during the few moments we face each other and determine our contribution to each other as we go by. Not running into each other constitutes the positive contributions we make to each other while we are in this very short relationship. Once we have passed each other, the interaction is complete. Our relationship is complete as well if we never see each other again.

Example: You are standing in line with a person in front of you. If you accept the fact that the person in front of you has a right to occupy that position in line and you do not try to occupy it yourself, then you are making the appropriate contribution for a level 1 relationship.

While this level of relationship maturity is adequate for motorists and pedestrians, it is inadequate in relationships that should function at higher levels, such as with family members, coworkers, friends, etc.

I am going to diagram the contributions of the **Relationship Maturity Model™™**. Level 1 is at the bottom and we will move up as the relationship become more mature.

The required contribution of level 1 is *acknowledgement*.

Relationship Maturity Model™

```
7 –
6 –
5 –
4 –
3 –
2 –
1 – Acknowledgement
```

Level 2

The maturity requirement of level 2 is *respect*. The contribution we will observe relationship partners making is *courtesy*.

This level of relationship maturity is adequate for interactions with people we generally do not know, but with whom we need to interact in order to conduct business, give or receive services, be social with, etc. For example, this is the level of maturity expected when interacting with the salesclerk at the grocery store, the bank teller, the customer support person on the phone, the receptionist at the doctor's office, co-workers in other departments of the company, etc.

Example: I step up to pay for my grocery items at the check-out register. The young lady greets me asking how I am.

"Fine, thank you, how are you?" I ask in reply.

"Fine, thank you. Did you find everything you needed?" she goes on.

"Yes, thank you."

"Do you have any plans for the weekend?" she asks.

I reply, "Yes, I think we will be going to the rodeo."

"Oh, that's nice. That will be $13.76, thank you."

After paying she wishes me a nice day.

She and I have just interacted at level 2 maturity.

Courtesy is a funny thing. The young lady asked how I was, but did she really want to know? I doubt it. When I asked her how she was, did I really want to know? Not really. Did she really want to know if I had found everything I needed? Probably not. What if I had answered in the negative, would that have prompted her to do anything other than empathize? I doubt it. I fully expect that her job tasks have been defined in such a way that she is expected to pose those questions as a token of being friendly and courteous.

Courtesy is not intended to be an actual exchange of important information, but instead to create a sense of ease, acceptance, and friendliness. It does this with very little effort. In a business situation, its purpose is to allow business to be transacted easily and efficiently and to encourage and invite the customer to return and conduct more business when the opportunity next presents itself. The same holds true for similar interactions in other situations or circumstances.

When you see relationship partners interacting and both are contributing *courtesy*, then you know that the relationship is functioning at the second level of maturity.

Relationship Maturity Model™

```
7 –
6 –
5 –
4 –
3 –
2 – Courtesy
1 – Acknowledgement
```

Level 3

The maturity requirement for level 3 is *to know*. The contribution you will observe relationship partners making is the *sharing of meaningful information*.

The first thing I need to point out is that each level of higher maturity builds on the previous ones. A relationship cannot function at level 3 if either of the relationship partners is unwilling to make the contributions required by levels 1 and 2.

Before we talk about meaningful information, I need to introduce another concept. We need to talk about *Personal Attributes* and *Personal Resources*.

Personal Attributes are those things that make you uniquely you. They are such things as your:

- Qualities
- Character traits
- Feelings
- Opinions
- Beliefs
- Emotions
- Virtues
- Likes and dislikes
- Knowledge
- Capabilities

Personal Resources are those things that you can give away, but they are things that only you can give. They include such things as your time, effort, energy, attention, consideration, and so forth.

Individually, a person is composed of his or her *personal attributes* and his or her *personal resources*. Both can be used as contributions in an interaction.

You have likely heard people talk about the third level of relationship maturity if you have heard phrases like "I don't know her that well," "It's time to get to know each other," or "This is a whole new side of you that I did not know about."

The observed contribution at this level is the sharing of *meaningful information*. This takes place when the relationship partners share personal attributes. They will be willing to share personal information about themselves with each other. It is meaningful because the things shared are valued elements of themselves. Getting to know someone happens at this level of relationship maturity.

If we use the example of making a friend, this level of maturity is a very natural next step right after the relationship partners acknowledge each other and have shown courtesy to each other.

By contrast, this level of relationship maturity goes too far for those relationships that are intended to operate at level 2. For example, in a customer/cashier relationship where level 2 maturity is very appropriate, level 3 could be viewed as inappropriate, concerning, awkward, and would probably be discouraged by store policy. This does not mean you cannot become friends, but it does mean that the relationship would need to be pursued outside of the work environment where level 2 contributions are expected.

Meaningful Information: Facts vs Personal Attributes

How can I recognize if the information being shared qualifies as being meaningful?

Initially, a person may consider facts to be meaningful information. For example, knowing the fact that water is made up of two hydrogen atoms and one oxygen atom seems like meaningful information, especially if I need to know it for a test at school or to accomplish something at work. However, sharing the atomic composition of water does not really help increase the maturity of a relationship.

Example: A teacher in a classroom setting states that water is composed of two hydrogen atoms and one oxygen atom.

In this scenario, the teacher is presenting facts that the student needs to learn to become more educated. The presentation of this fact in and of itself has no impact on the teacher/student relationship. In fact, many teaching and training interactions function quite adequately at level 2, so sharing these facts, as far as relationship maturity is concerned, is not the meaningful information required for level 3 maturity.

Now consider this example: My son comes running into my office and announces, with great enthusiasm, that water is made up of two hydrogen atoms and one oxygen atom.

In this interaction, is my son contributing at level 2 or level 3?

He is contributing at level 3. His contribution has nothing to do with atoms or water, but it has everything to do with the excitement he feels from learning something new. It is something he is proud of and he wants to share his accomplishment with me. What did he just share? He shared several of his personal attributes and used the atomic composition of water to do it.

What attributes did he share? At the very least, he shared his emotion of excitement, his feelings of accomplishment, and his positive self-view as he realizes he is capable of learning something significant. Now go back to the list of personal attributes listed above and pick them out: *emotions*, *feelings*, and *capabilities*. Any one of them would be enough to qualify as a contribution of meaningful information. In this example, he shared at least three and maybe more.

What should my response be so that I am contributing at level 3 as well? How about: "Son, that's great! I am proud of you." Did I share personal attributes? Yes, I shared my emotions and my feelings.

As I described these events, you have been a virtual outside observer watching this interaction play out. You watched my son have an interaction with me in which he shared meaningful information composed of personal attributes and then you saw me respond with a contribution of personal attributes as well. What can you conclude from your observations? You can conclude, at least for this interaction, that our relationship was functioning at maturity level 3. If you could watch our interactions over the next few days and if you saw a consistent pattern of interactions with level 3 contributions, then you could conclude with confidence that the relationship between me and my son is stable and consistent at level 3 maturity.

This level of relationship maturity is very appropriate for social events, working with professionals such as doctors, neighbors, associations with members of groups or religious organizations, etc.

Relationship Maturity Model™

```
7 –
6 –
5 –
4 –
3 – Meaningful Information
2 – Courtesy
1 – Acknowledgement
```

Some Observations

Prior to describing the first maturity level, I told you that I would show you how to measure relationship strength, how to measure demand weight, and how to match the two.

I have walked you through the first three levels of relationship maturity showing you that it can be measured by the level of contribution the relationship partners are willing to contribute in their interactions with each other. This is also how you measure the weight of a demand. A demand that requires the contribution of acknowledgement is a very light demand. One that requires the contribution of personal attributes is heavier, relatively speaking.

As we proceed through the remaining levels of relationship maturity, you will see that the contributions become more significant. The demands these contributions can satisfy will also become heavier.

I also explained that there are types of relationships that function adequately at each of these first three levels without the expectation of increasing in maturity. I have also explained that these first three levels are a natural progression for those relationships that can and should function at higher levels.

Understanding this, I can now introduce the fourth law of the **Principle of Relationship Maturity**.

IV. A relationship develops by progressing through the levels of maturity until arriving at the level appropriate for that relationship.

We have seen examples of this in the first three levels. We will see more examples with the remaining levels of maturity.

I need to explain one more thing. Interactions between two people may hop around a bit. You may observe two people interacting at level 3. They may have an interaction where level 2 contributions are made, then subsequent interactions will be back at 3, then at 1, and so forth. This is not unusual, and it should not cause alarm. Some interactions may only require level 2 contributions and some only level 1. If you have observed the partners functioning at level 3 with level 3 contributions, then the thing you are looking for is whether the relationship is consistently and comfortably functioning at level 3 over time. If so, then the relationship is stable at that level and I would fully expect to see the partners enjoying the associated benefits.

Homework assignment:

1. Start observing.

2. See if you can identify contributions that are being made in interactions.

3. See if you can identify what level of maturity a given interaction employs and then, if you can, make a series of observations over time to see if you can determine if the relationship is stable at a given level of maturity.

4. Keep a journal and note interesting observations and insights.

Let's move to the next level of the **Relationship Maturity Model™**.

Level 4

The maturity requirement: *To Meet Partner Demands*

Observable contribution: *Personal Resources*

Partner demands. As a relationship moves to level 4 the partners will continue to have interactions with each other. One partner will bring a want and the other partner will respond to that want. What makes level 4 different from the previous levels is that the partners will now bring a new type of want to their interactions. These new wants will need a responding contribution of *personal resources* from the other partner. When you see partners contributing personal resources in their interactions, you will know that the relationship is functioning at level 4.

Remember, personal resources are things that only you can give such as time, energy, attention, and so forth.

Some people will ask, "It seems that personal resources, particularly time, were spent in responding to interactions at the previous three levels. Isn't that true?" The answer is yes. Limited expenditures of personal resources were used in the previous three levels. However, level 4 requires a substantially greater expenditure of personal resources on a consistent basis than what was previously needed. For example, going on a date requires level 4 contributions. The date may take 3 or 4 hours. That type of expenditure is not typical for the previous three levels. Additional personal resources, as well as time, would also be contributed at level 4 which would not be expended at the lower levels.

Example: In a budding romantic relationship, level 4 would be characterized by dating, spending time together, and doing things together.

Example: In a supervisor/employee relationship, level 4 would be characterized by demands that the two relationship partners would place on each other such as the giving and accepting of assignments, giving status reports, doing training, and a host of other things.

Relationship Maturity Model™

```
7 –
6 –
5 –
4 – Personal Resources
3 – Meaningful Information
2 – Courtesy
1 – Acknowledgement
```

Homework assignment:

1. See if you can identify relationships functioning at level 4.

2. What personal resources are the two partners contributing?

Level 5

The maturity requirement: *To Meet Partnership Demands*

Observable contribution: *Partnership resources*

Partnership demands are those demands that require a response from the partnership and partnership assets.

While a relationship is functioning at Level 4, the partners were learning how to meet demands together by placing demands on each other. Equally important during this time they were learning about the personal attributes and the personal resources that are available to the relationship. They were exploring and identifying their collective set of assets. These assets of personal attributes and personal resources are now partnership resources and can be used to meet partnership demands.

Meeting partnership demands can be accomplished in a variety of ways. Meeting them may require that both partners work together, it may require that one partner focuses on some demands while the other focuses on the remaining demands, it may require a tag-team approach, etc. When partners work together to meet partnership demands, the relationship is functioning at level 5.

The following are examples of relationships that function at level 5 listed by type of relationship:

- *Romantic relationships* – Engagement and marriage

- *Business relationships* – Collaborative efforts, joint accomplishments

- *Friendships* – Friends that function at level 5 are committed to each other, are there for each other during challenges, and do more together than the occasional social event. Not all friendships function at level 5.

- *Sibling relationships* – Not all sibling relationships function here, but they can. An example would be when siblings rally to face a challenge together.

- *Marriage* – Marriages should function at level 5, but not all do.

Example: Let's say that Tyler and Emily have been dating and yesterday they got engaged. This new circumstance brings a host of new partnership demands they need to address. One partner may be assigned to make the response, but the response applies to the partnership because both partners are subject to it. These demands include such things as setting a date for the wedding, picking a location, identifying where they will live after the wedding, choosing a honeymoon, selecting guests, sending out invitations, and on and on the list goes.

Marriage is another relationship that deals with partnership demands. These demands include such things as the couple supporting themselves, providing for a place to live, paying bills, providing transportation for themselves, and so forth.

Relationship Maturity Model™

```
7 –
6 –
5 – Partnership Resources
4 – Personal Resources
3 – Meaningful Information
2 – Courtesy
1 – Acknowledgement
```

Level 6

The maturity requirement: *Create Our Own Demands*

Observable contribution: *Commitment and Meeting the Demands as a Team*

Level 6 requires a significant investment of personal attributes and personal resources before the relationship can function at this level in a sustainable fashion. Be aware that while a relationship can be expected to function at this level, not all do.

Relationships that can function at level 6:

- *Romantic relationships* – Marriages can and eventually should function here.

- *Employment relationships* – The relationships that exist between the members of a seasoned team. These are somewhat rare, but they do exist.

- *Business relationships* – A committed, entrepreneurial partnership

- *Sports and military teams* – Sports clubs sometimes function here; military teams often function here particularly demonstration teams like the Blue Angels.

Create Our Own Demands. Instead of being reactive to the demands that come, my partner and I are going to choose to impose upon ourselves a demand or set of demands and we are going to commit to meeting those demands as a team.

In a marriage, examples include deciding to have a baby, deciding to alter a lifestyle or life circumstances in order to accept a new job opportunity, supporting each other in the pursuit of personal or couple interests or goals, and so forth.

Commitment: In a level 6 relationship, the relationship partners commit to accepting and responding individually and collectively to demands that they have chosen to pursue. They are committing to each other to support each other by take up the slack if the other has to focus more on the new demands, they are committing to not abandoning the other partner or the relationship under the increased demand load, and they are committing to not allowing the relationship to weaken while the new demand load is being addressed.

This is, in part, the definition of a team.

Team. Both partners commit to the following approach: Each partner assumes full responsibility for themselves and for their partner. This is the territory of focused attention on incremental improvements to capture the last few percentage points of complete unity in the relationship. A team knows that it takes daily attention and a regular alignment to the higher wants of self-imposed demands. It is the mentality that you are an extension of me and I of you. We know each other so well and have worked long enough together that we know what the other will do in a given circumstance and we each can depend on that response. We rarely encounter a mismatch of expectations.

When a relationship is functioning at Level 6, we will observe the partners stepping outside of their comfort levels to achieve more and to become more. They will work together towards the goals they have set for themselves. They will be willing to take on more work, responsibility, and obligations to achieve their goals. They will have a clear vision of where they want to go and a well-thought-out plan on how to get there. They will be committed to each other, to the relationship, and to their vision of the future. They will work very well together and will appear to know each other extremely well.

Relationship Maturity Model™

7 –
6 – Commitment
5 – Partnership Resources
4 – Personal Resources
3 – Meaningful Information
2 – Courtesy
1 – Acknowledgement

Level 7

The maturity requirement: *Selflessness*

Observable contribution: *Selfless Service*

A good example is the parent/child relationship. The spousal relationship can also function at this level, but it usually requires years of investment to achieve.

Selfless Service. The definition of selfless service is to do for other people what they cannot do for themselves and do it with no thought for yourself.

Relationship Maturity Model™

7 – Selfless Service
6 – Commitment
5 – Partnership Resources
4 – Personal Resources
3 – Meaningful Information
2 – Courtesy
1 – Acknowledgement

Homework assignment:

1. See if you can find examples of people functioning at level 6 or 7.

2. Make notes in your journal of what you observe and any insights you gain.

Notes

CHAPTER V

Strengthening a Relationship

You now know how to measure relationship strength and demand weight. Now I am going to show you how to use that understanding to strengthen a relationship. I will begin by introducing the remaining three laws of the **Principle of Relationship Maturity**.

V. *Any attempt or expectation to get your partner to skip a contribution level will produce disruption in the relationship, distrust, and distance between the partners.*

VI. *The only way to invite a relationship partner to contribute at a higher level is to start contributing there first. This creates the perfect invitation without violating any principles.*

VII. *Both partners must be willingly contributing at a given maturity level before the relationship can declare that it is functioning at that level.*

Let's look at each law in detail.

V. Any attempt or expectation to get your partner to skip a contribution level will produce disruption in the relationship, distrust, and distance between the partners.

This means that if I am trying to build a relationship with someone and then if I get overenthusiastic or impatient and create an attempt or expectation to get my partner to skip a contribution level, my attempt will disrupt the relationship and undermine the progress we have been making. As a result, my relationship partner will start to distance himself or herself from me by reducing his or her level of contributions.

I am going to tell you a short story to illustrate this law.

John is a student at a large university. One day he is walking across campus and sees a beautiful young lady headed toward a line. He follows and gets in line right behind her. After a few moments he asks her what the purpose of the line is and explains that his experience has taught him if there is a line, it is usually one he needs to be in. She finds his comment somewhat amusing and explains that it is a line to get concert tickets. He asks who is playing and she explains. John expresses interest in the band and over the next twenty minutes he has a nice conversation with Sarah, whose name he learned after the first few minutes of talking. While in line, they talk about school, classes, home, family, and tastes in music. Just prior to getting tickets he asks who will be going with her to the concert. She explains that her roommates have other plans so she will be going alone. John musters some courage and asks her if she would mind going with him to the concert. She agrees, to his surprise and relief. He gets her address and sets a time to pick her up. As they go their separate ways, John reflects on what just happened and is very pleased.

The night of the concert he picks her up and they have a lovely evening talking, laughing, and enjoying the music. After the concert John takes her back to her apartment. He walks her to the door and says, "I have just had the most amazing evening. I would like to thank you for that. It has been such a long time since I have enjoyed myself this much and it's all because of you. I just feel so comfortable around you. It is almost as if we have known each other for years. In fact, this has been so amazing that I am confident that we really are meant for each other. Sarah, will you marry me?" Sarah stares at him a moment without responding, then she tells him that she had a nice time, thanks him, and goes into her apartment.

Over the next few days he tries several times to call Sarah, but each time one of her roommates answers the phone and explains that Sarah is busy or not there. On the fourth day he happens to see her on the other side of the cafeteria. He calls out to her and waves. He catches her eye and she sheepishly waves back and then darts out the door.

That is the end of the story so let's talk about it. When I am face to face with people telling the story, they chuckle, laugh, or gasp when I get to the marriage proposal. I usually pause the story for a moment while I ask them why they are reacting that way. They give all kinds of reasons including that it was stupid thing to do, it did not feel right, it was not the right time, etc. We all have a built-in sense that what he did was not going to get a positive response from Sarah. I then ask if anyone knows why things fell apart with John and Sarah. It is because he skipped a level of relationship maturity.

Let's go back and see how things progressed and then how things digressed.

He was obviously at level 1 when he stepped in line behind her.

He started a conversation and she answered, most likely, out of courtesy. Where are they now? Yes, level 2.

Over the course of the next twenty minutes what did they talk about? Lots of personal things. Where are they now? Level 3. Both are voluntarily sharing meaningful information in the form of personal attributes.

Just before buying tickets he asks her to go to the concert with him. He just invited her to spend time with him. That was a level 4 invitation and she agreed.

They go to the concert. They are both contributing time, energy, effort, and attention as they have a good time there. These are level 4 contributions and they are solidly functioning there.

Then he proposed. What level of contribution was he going after? He was asking for Level 6 – Commitment. He skipped 5.

Now what happens? She starts a systematic retreat down the levels of maturity. She was at 4, but then at the door she says that she had a nice time to close the conversation and then goes inside. She shared how she felt. That is a level 3 contribution and the fact that she said anything at all before going inside could be counted as a brief expression of courtesy. I would say she is quickly passing through 3 and headed to 2. Over the next few days it becomes obvious that she does not want to talk to him and then when she sees him, she acknowledges his wave, but then darts out of the room. She contributed at 2, barely, and is headed for 1.

From this story we can understand a couple of things:

It is possible to move up through the levels of maturity quite quickly. You cannot expect it to always happen that way, but it is possible.

Skipping a level really does cause disruption in the relationship, halts progress, and introduces distance between the partners. Sarah retreated down the levels as fast of faster than she had ascended them. With each descending step she introduced more distance between John and herself.

Improving a Relationship

You now have enough information to improve a relationship. I told you at the beginning of the book that I organized this book to give you a tool you could use to improve a relationship if you would commit to getting to *Chapter 5*. Well, you have arrived, so I will explain what the tool is and how to use it.

If you are in a relationship that is strained, in one that is struggling, or even in one that you would like to improve, this next section will show you how to do that. The way it is done is by applying the principles we have been discussing.

I am going to tell you another story to illustrate how it is done.

I met with a father who was struggling with his teenage son. He explained that his son would not clean his room, would attend school only periodically, rarely did his homework, and went on to explain several other challenges he was having with him. He said that he had tried numerous times to talk to his son trying to get him to do the things he was supposed to do, but his son would not engage. He had tried grounding him, taking away privileges, and offering rewards, but nothing worked.

I asked if his son ever called him names. He said, "No."

Why would I ask that? Because I wanted to determine the level of contribution his son was willing to give. The answer I got from the father suggested that the son might be willing to contribute at level 2—*courtesy*.

I explained the **Relationship Maturity Model™** to the father and asked him to identify at what level of contribution he felt his son was willing to contribute. He narrowed it down to either 1 or 2. I suggested that we might assume 2. I then asked, "At what level are you expecting him to contribute?" After thinking about it he finally suggested that he was expecting contributions at level 4 because he wanted his son to contribute personal resources (time, energy, attention, etc.). I told him that I would agree.

So, if you are expecting this level (I held my hand horizontally about eye height), but he is willing to contribute only at this level (I held my other hand horizontally at about chest height), what do you think the problem is?

He caught the idea of it almost immediately. "We are expecting different things," he said.

"You're right," I responded. "Your expectations are mismatched."

Then I asked, "As you continue to push to have him to contribute at 4, how do you think he will respond?"

The father replied, "He will pull back more and more."

"Is that what you have been seeing?" I asked.

The father nodded.

He thought about it for a minute and then asked, "So what do I do?"

I explained that if his son is only willing to contribute at level 2 when interacting with you, then you have to go to level 2, have some interactions there where nothing more is expected other than level 2 contributions, and stabilize your relationship.

Let's pause the story for a moment. What does an interaction look like at level 2? Referring to the **Relationship Maturity Model™** we find *courtesy* is the contribution at that level. How would you conduct an interaction where courtesy is the desired contribution? Remember that both the want and the response to the want are contributions. If you are going to initiate an interaction and the contribution expectation is courtesy, then what do you need to want? This is what the father needed to change. He needed to want to have an interaction where he contributed courtesy and hoped to receive it back.

Let's go back to the story. The father and I talked about it a bit more and then the father decided on a plan. He would go past his son's room and ask him how his day was going. I told him that was a good plan. So that is what he did. The son responded as expected saying that it was fine. The father responded with, "That's great," and then left the room. He had just had an interaction with his son in which both contributions were courtesy.

The father had additional interactions with him over the course of the next few days where courtesy was the desired objective. Each interaction was successful although he noted that his son had somewhat of a puzzled look on his face as the interactions went on.

The puzzled look was because of the track record the father had established up until now. He had been trying to use tactics to get his son to function at level 4, but these most recent interactions did not appear to have a tactic or hidden agenda associated with them, at least that the son could discover, and so he was not entirely sure he trusted these encounters. He was wondering if this was some new tactic that he could not yet figure out.

The mistrust on the son's part is completely expected. Trust in their relationship was in tatters and had to be rebuilt. The beauty of applying principles is that trust is a natural byproduct.

After a few days of successful interactions, I explained the following method for improving the strength or maturity of their relationship.

The father needs to strengthen the relationship before he can place level 4 contribution demands on it. When the relationship is functioning at level 2, it is not strong enough to support the weight of higher level demands.

Strengthening Methodology

You now have the information you need to improve a relationship. Let's talk about how it is done.

When you want to strengthen a relationship, you must go through these steps.

First, identify the level at which your relationship partner is willing to contribute.

Second, initiate a series of interactions where the ONLY objective is to have both partners make that level of contribution. Continue initiating these interactions until the relationship stabilizes. Be patient. Sometimes this make take a while depending upon how mangled the trust is.

Third, when the relationship has stabilized, invite your relationship partner to the next level of maturity. The only way this can be done is by going there first and making the appropriate contribution.

Fourth, continue initiating interactions with this objective until your relationship partner responds with the same level of contribution. Then go back to step one and start again.

I explained to the father that he was going to have to go through this process two times successfully in order to get the relationship to level 4.

I also cautioned him to absolutely resist the temptation to skip a level when things appear to be improving. This happens frequently and is devastating to the relationship because it is so destructive to trust. Stick with the process and be patient.

Once I was sure he understood the process, we spent some time talking about what level 3 contributions look like. I reminded him that this was the level of meaningful information and the sharing of personal attributes.

The trap some people fall into is their perception of what success looks like at level 3. They think that the invitation should be composed of questions to try and get their relationship partner to share meaningful information with them. However, remember step three in the strengthening methodology? The most effective invitation is to initiate an interaction and share meaningful information first.

Continuing my story, the father told me the following:

I knew he liked music that I knew very little about. However, it was not too hard to find out who some of these bands were and what songs they played. I did some research and found a couple songs and listened to them a few times. I chose one and then selected a line in the song that had some meaning to me. I then watched for an opportunity to have an interaction. Our interactions at level 2 had been going well so I decided to invite him to interact at level 3. I had to take the first step and I knew that the best invitation was to share meaningful information with him. When the opportunity for the interaction came, I simply said that I had come across this song and I told him the part of the lyrics that I liked. He stared at me for a moment and then said, "But Dad, you don't like that kind of music." I replied, "I am trying to branch out." I was prepared to stop there, but then he said, "Have you listened to any other songs by that band?" I responded, "Yes, I have also heard this other song," and I named it. My son was even more surprised at that, but then started telling me about other songs I should listen to. I wrote them down and said that I would.

When the father told me that, I grabbed his shoulder and exclaimed, "Perfect!" He had just navigated a very successful level 3 interaction. I encouraged him to use the methodology we had discussed and to stabilize the relationship at 3. He said he would and that he had several more ideas that he wanted to pursue to do just that.

A few weeks later the father told me that he had just invited his son to level 4 and that his son had responded positively. The father was thrilled.

This story illustrates the correct application of the principles. Let's talk about the sixth law.

VI. The only way to invite a relationship partner to contribute at a higher level is to start contributing there first. This creates the perfect invitation without violating any principles.

We saw this law at work in the story.

I hope you can see the difference between asking questions to try and get your partner to share meaningful information and sharing meaningful information first. While it appears that asking questions is a show of interest, you are actually asking your partner to contribute at level 3 before you are willing to do it. Pushing your partner to a higher level from a lower one vs. helping pull him up to that level because you are already there are two approaches that will get vastly different responses.

Once a relationship stabilizes at a given level, the only way to create the perfect invitation to make a greater contribution in an interaction is by going there first. Notice that I keep using the word *invitation*. This is because your partner can only make a contribution in an interaction voluntarily, otherwise you will violate the first **Principle of Relationships** which is the **Principle of Choice**.

Also remember, if trust is weak, it may take a number of invitations before your relationship partner will respond accordingly. Be patient and just keep inviting. If you have an interaction in which you make the invitation, but your partner does not respond to it, then have a few more interactions at the current level of contribution before trying again. It is vitally important that you do not accidentally initiate an interaction that skips a level. If you do, you will erase all your progress almost instantly.

Purpose of Strengthening a Relationship

The relationship has started to improve between the father and son. Remember that the father said that the son would not do the things his father asked.

Will improving the relationship help with all the challenges the father described earlier? The answer is yes, but not automatically.

The things the father was asking his son to do represent placing demands that one relationship partner is asking the other to do. This requires level 4 contributions in the **Relationship Maturity Model™**. If the father places these demands on his son prior to the relationship being mature enough to support the demands, then the son is going to retreat and will start taking or making opportunities to introduce distance into the relationship. The first thing that must be done to make the situation better is to focus on strengthening the relationship. The relationship has to be strong enough to support the demands that will be placed on it. The demands of cleaning his room and doing chores requires level 4 relationship strength.

There is a law that supports and guides this process. It is the seventh and final law of the **Principle of Relationship Maturity**.

VII. Both partners must be willingly contributing at a given maturity level before the relationship can declare that it is functioning at that level.

In the case of the father/son story, this means that both the father and the son must be willingly contributing, not just willing to contribute, but willingly and actively contributing at level 4 before the relationship is functioning at that level. If the father is doing all the asking and the son is doing all the work, then this relationship is not functioning at level 4. That type of an approach will produce strained interactions and distance between the partners because the seventh law of this principle has been applied incorrectly. From the definition, both partners must be willingly contributing which means that some of the interactions between the father and the son will be father initiated with the son responding and it means that there has to be level 4 contributions being made by the father in response to son initiated demands.

Here is a summary of the Relationship Strengthening Methodology:

First: Identify the level at which your relationship partner is willing to contribute.

Second: Initiate a series of interactions where the ONLY objective is to have both partners make that level of contribution. Continue initiating these interactions until the relationship stabilizes. Be patient. Sometimes this make take a while depending upon how beat up the trust is.

Third: When the relationship has stabilized, invite your relationship partner to the next level of maturity by going there first and making the appropriate contribution.

Fourth: Continue initiating interactions with this objective until your relationship partner responds with the same level of contribution. Then go back to step one and start again.

You now have everything you need to start doing something to improve a struggling relationship. The **Relationship Maturity Model™** and the **Relationship Strengthening Methodology** are powerful tools. They can make a huge difference in your relationship in a relatively short amount of time.

Homework assignment:

1. Remember to be patient. Trust might be in pretty bad shape.

2. Be consistent. These are not tools you only use on weekends. Once you start using them, keep using them. If you are inconsistent, you will make any improvement even harder to achieve.

3. Plan your interactions. Know exactly the contribution you will make and the one you are hoping your partner will make before you interact.

4. Plan of how you will invite your relationship partner to the next level.

5. Keep a journal, record observations and insights.

Notes

CHAPTER VI

Interactions

The interaction is the very heart of a successful relationship. Interactions construct the *fabric of a relationship* and it is by means of interactions that *the repairing qualities contained within the principles are delivered to the very soul of relationships.*

I have shown you how to create greater strength in your relationship by increasing maturity. You do this by stabilizing your relationship where happens to be and then inviting your relationship partner to make greater contributions in your interactions. You can strengthen your relationships very effectively as long as you have productive interactions.

What we need to do now is focus on what is required to have productive interactions. I am going to show you how to effectively guide your interactions to productive conclusions.

In the examples I have been giving thus far, the interactions have been productive and so the examples have worked out nicely.

Unfortunately, interactions do not always head down a productive path. Unproductive interactions undermine the relationship. They weaken and will eventually destroy trust, they abuse the partners, they burn holes in the fabric of the relationship, and they produce distance between the relationship partners.

The governing **Principles of Relationships** are powerful enough to repair damaged relationships, but they will have little effect if the interactions are not productive. Therefore, the next topic we need to discuss is how interactions work, how to guide them to a productive conclusion, and what to do if you find yourself in the middle of unproductive interactions.

This discussion depends on understanding the fourth governing **Principles of Relationships**. This is the **Principle of Unity**. This principle is composed of five laws. I will start by introducing the first four laws. The fifth one will come later.

I. *Successful relationships naturally produce unity between the relationship partners.*
II. *Capacity for greater unity increases with relationship maturity.*
III. *The opposite of unity is distance.*
IV. *An interaction will always produce an incremental increase in unity or distance.*

Let's examine each of these laws.

Unity is the bringing together of diverse parts into a united whole.

Unity is the state of being one. When two people become unified, they achieve a synergy which can be described as the whole being greater than the sum of its parts. Two people, unified and united in a relationship, can achieve greater things than would be possible for either of them working individually and separately.

Being unified does not mean that relationship partners must feel the same things, like the same things, or do the same things. The purpose of unity is not to create identical twins out of the relationship partners. Unity thrives on the diversity the two partners bring to a relationship. Two people, truly unified in a relationship are one in purpose and are united in wants, goals, and objectives that support their purpose.

A relationship has greater capacity for unity as it increases in maturity. Remember that there are relationships that function appropriately at each level of relationship maturity, i.e. motorists and pedestrians at level 1, conducting business with the general public at level 2, and so forth. Each level of maturity has the capacity of producing a certain level of unity. As maturity increases, so does the capacity to achieve a greater or higher level of unity.

For example, the unity available at level 2 needs to be enough to accomplish the business at hand. The two people engaged in a common effort are unified in working through those things that are required to conclude the business transaction. You can come away from a successful transaction feeling that you have experienced unity in the objective. By contrast, you can also experience the frustration of trying to transact business with a person who is not interested or engaged in the same purpose.

This level of unity is vastly different, for example, than the unity experienced by two people who have decided to have a baby and are committed to raising their child to maturity.

The opposite of unity is distance. Distance can be both observed and felt. It will manifest itself in some or all the following ways: the introduction of physical space between partners, a reduction in the level of contributions given while interacting, a reduced willingness to contribute, and a reduction in trust.

Every interaction produces results. These results will be experienced in the following forms:

1. Satisfying the original want
2. A feeling indicating success or failure of the interaction
3. An incremental increase in unity or distance.

If the interaction was productive, then it will produce an incremental increase in unity which will be felt by the relationship partners. If the interaction was unproductive or unsuccessful, then the result will be an incremental increase in distance which will also be felt by the partners.

Now let's take a more detailed look at the interaction itself.

The Five Events of an Interaction

In Chapter 3, I introduced the **Principle of Interactions.**

The second law of interactions is: *An interaction is composed of five events. These events transpire the same way every time, everywhere, for everyone.*

The third law of interactions is: *Each event has a participation requirement. How a person responds to the participation requirements in an interaction determines how productive or unproductive the interaction will be.*

You will recall that the event requirements are *Partner, Choose, Learn, Contribute*, and *Check.*

The fourth law of interactions is: *There are only three possible responses to each participation requirement. One response is correct and will produce good results. The other two responses are counterfeits and can only produce poor results.*

There are only *three* ways to respond to each participation requirement — only *three*.

I am stressing this point because it is huge! It means that an interaction is not some great and complex thing. It is manageable. Anyone can do it and be successful.

Of the three response choices available, only one is correct and capable of producing positive results. Again, this is huge! It means that there are not fifty or a hundred possible ways to respond and I don't have to sift through them all trying to determine which is going to be right. There are only three response choices and only one of them is correct.

The other two response choices are counterfeits. A counterfeit has the appearance of being able to produce good results but is incapable of doing so.

The correct response at each interaction event leads to a productive interaction which produces more unity in the relationship.

The counterfeit responses results in an unproductive interaction which produces distance in the relationship.

I will refer to a person who responds correctly to the participation requirements as going Center Path.

I will refer to a person choosing one or the other of the counterfeits as going North or going South.

Let's first go through the interaction events and look at Center Path responses.

Center Path

Going Center Path means responding to each of the interaction participation requirements with exactly what is required. I will identify the requirement and then the correct response.

An interaction requires the participation of two people. I will refer to them as the initiating partner and the responding partner. In three events both partners do the same thing and in two events they do slightly different things, although what they do is very closely related. I will note the differences as they arise.

The following are the interaction participation requirements and the Center Path responses.

Interaction Road Map™

Partner: I attribute equal worth

Choose: Initiating partner -- I invite participation
　　　　　Responding partner -- I choose to participate

Learn: I seek understanding

Contribute: Responding partner -- I gift my contribution
　　　　　Initiating partner -- I receive the gift

Check: I check results and attribute worth

Let's look at each event and Center Path response in more detail.

First Event: The requirement is to form the partnership. The initiating partner decides what kind of partnership he or she wants to form for the interaction. That determination is made by assessing how he or she views his or her partner. There are three options. Using myself as the example, I can view my partner as beneath me, equal with me, or above me.

The Center Path response is to view or position my partner on the same plane or equal with me. The way to do that is to *attribute equal worth* to my partner. I accomplish that by assessing my own self-worth and then attributing or viewing my partner as having that same amount.

By contrast, if I were going North, I would view my partner as having less worth than I have. I view myself as taking a position above my partner.

If I were going South, I would view my partner as having more worth than I do. I might conclude that my partner is better than me, more important than me, etc. I will view myself as being positioned below my partner.

This positioning is the most critical factor in determining the outcome of the interaction. If Center Path is not chosen at the outset, then the interaction is already on North or South footing and will continue to an unproductive conclusion.

The obvious question is: What if I go Center Path, but my partner does not, is the interaction doomed?

The answer is "no." Application of the principles is powerful enough to produce positive results even if only one partner is willing to apply them. You can guide an interaction a productive outcome by going Center Path. I am going to talk much more about this later in the book.

The initiating partner will determine his or her position before starting the interaction. The moment the interaction begins, the responding partner will determine his or her position. Independent of when positioning takes place in the timeline of the interaction, Center Path positioning is to *attribute equal worth – I attribute the same worth to you as I do myself.*

Second Event: The requirement is to choose. Here the initiating partner and responding partner participate in the interaction with slight differences. The initiating partner introduces the want in this event. The Center

Path action for the initiating partner is to invite participation. The Center Path response for the responding partner is to make a participation choice. Going Center Path does not mean that you always do what your partner wants. Your partner may present a want that would be detrimental to either or both partners or to the relationship. However, if addressing the want or just simply participating in the interaction would be beneficial to either partner or to the relationship, then choosing to participate would be going Center Path. The idea being that an opportunity to invest in the relationship is a better choice than being lazy or indifferent.

Third Event: The requirement is to learn. The want presented by the initiating partner is likely the product of a demand he or she may be facing and he or she is asking for help. If I am the responding partner, this is all new information and I need to come up to speed so that I can offer effective assistance. I may already possess the information and understanding needed to respond to the want or I may need to acquire more in order to formulate the best contribution to the interaction. The Center Path response for this event is to seek understanding. This applies equally to both partners.

Fourth Event: The requirement is to contribute. Here again, the requirements are slightly different for the two partners, but in both cases the required action is associated to a contribution. The Center Path response for the responding partner is to make his or her contribution to the interaction by doing what he or she can to satisfy the want presented by the initiating partner. Making the contribution is only part of the requirement. The way he or she contributes is also part of the requirement. The contribution needs to be *gifted* to the initiating partner. The initiating partner need to receive the contribution as a *gift*. The reason both partners need to view the contribution as a gift is because the contribution must come with no hidden agendas, ulterior motives, or expectations. An ulterior motive is one that is intentionally hidden so that it is not obvious. The contribution needs to be contributed as a gift and receive it as such.

Fifth Event: The requirement is the same for both partners. It is to check results. Every interaction produces results in several areas, one of which is in an incremental increase in unity or distance. The Center Path response for both partners is to check the results and see if the interaction produced an incremental increase in unity or an increase in distance. As they check results, they also attribute worth as they did in the first event. Worth comes when partners are able to work together, have a successful interaction, and enjoy an incremental increase in unity in a relationship that produces good things for both of them. One of the most common ways of attributing worth is gratitude.

The incremental increase in unity or distance will be felt. Interactions always produce feelings. People do not always pay close attention when the feelings are positive. This is typically because a positive conclusion to the interaction was what they expected. However, people are usually more aware of these feelings when they are negative.

Productive interactions will produce feelings that are often described as comfortable, content, satisfied, peaceful, etc. When the interaction is not productive, people typically describe feeling awkward, uncomfortable, unsettled, or confused. They often describe a desire to introduce some form of distance between themselves and the other person. That distance could be physical such as, "I don't want to sit quite so close to you" or "I am done interacting with you and I am leaving the room," or it could be emotional, such as, "I don't trust you," "I am going to be a bit more guarded or careful if we interact again," etc.

It is not a coincidence that attributing worth happens in both the first event and the last one in an interaction. The reason is because interactions should be viewed as cyclical. As you finish one interaction you are primed and ready for the next one.

Center Path responses may seem quite obvious. This is true until they are compared to the counterfeits. The contrast is quite telling. Let's talk about the two counterfeit options that are associated with each event.

Counterfeits

Remember that counterfeits have the appearance of being able to produce good results, but in the end, they are not capable of doing so.

There are two counterfeit responses opposing each Center Path response. These counterfeits can be grouped into a set called *going North* and another set called *going South*.

Going North

Going North is characterized by the belief that I can alter the participation requirements to suit my needs.

Going North looks like this:

Interaction Road Map™

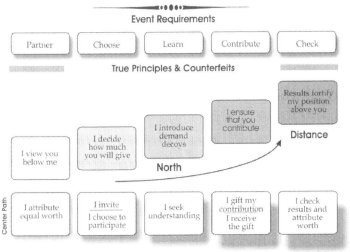

© 2019 Gary Moe

Partner: I view you below me

Choose: I decide how much you will give

Learn: I introduce demand decoys

Contribute: I ensure that you contribute

Check: Results fortify my position above you

Initially, this sounds very harsh, but you will be surprised by how subtle this approach can be and how often it is employed. Let's look at it in more detail.

Partner requirement: When it is time to form the partnership, the initiating partner makes the assessment that he or she is better than the other partner. Most of the time it is the initiating partner who decides to go North, but it could be either partner. If I were going North, I would conclude that I am better than my partner and I would draw that conclusion because I am comparing something between the two of us. The options I can choose from to justify my position are nearly endless. Some examples are: I am smarter, I am older, my title is greater, I was here first, I dress better, my hair is nicer, I am slimmer, I am a man, I am a woman, I have more money, I have a bigger house, I have a higher degree, I work harder, you are not as good as me, your behavior is unacceptable, I don't like you, I am more popular, my clothes are more expensive, and the list goes on and on and on. I am sure you get the idea.

It makes absolutely no difference how I justify going North. If I decide to go North, I will choose something as justification that allows me to declare, "I am better than you, therefore, I view you below me." Once I put myself in a position superior to you, then I have set the stage for everything that follows.

The primary reason I have for going North is to ensure that my want will be satisfied. Essentially, I am saying that my wants are more important than your wants, but I need you to help me get what I want.

Choose requirement: The requirement is to invite you to participate. If I am going North, I want to make your participation choice for you because I need your help in order to get what I want, so I choose that you will participate. I will start making your choices for you now because I also anticipating the fourth event when I will be choosing how much you will be expected to give when it is time for you to make your contribution.

You will probably notice that this approach flies directly in opposition to the first **Principle of Relationships** which is that everyone has the freedom to choose. If I am going North, my focus is on how I can get what I want. Leaving choice in your hands could have a detrimental effect on my goal, so I will try to remove that obstacle.

Learn requirement: The participation requirement is to learn about what is needed. Since I already know what is needed, I do not want learning to take place, so to maintain control my strategy is to keep you occupied on things that best serve my purpose. I will introduce demand decoys.

A demand decoy is something that takes attention from where it really needs to be and places it on something else. Going North, my want dominates. I need your help to get what I want, but to do so, I need your cooperation. My want is going to be self-serving and one-sided which may seriously jeopardize your cooperation if you spend any time really looking at it, so I am going to draw your attention away from that and put it somewhere else. I know this strategy will work well to help me get what I want. The tools of this strategy are decoys.

These are some examples of demand decoys:

- Guilt
- History
- Baggage
- Emotions
- Pretend facts
- Anger
- Blame
- Changing the subject
- Proving a point
- Comparisons
- Positional power
- Silence
- Withholding
- Holding the relationship hostage
- Being the martyr
- Excuses
- Tantrums
- Keeping score
- Blackmail
- Rewards
- Punishments

These are just a few examples. Some demand decoys can get very creative. We are going to talk more about these a little later.

Contribute requirement: It is now time for the contribution. Everything I have been doing thus far was in anticipation of getting here. It is now time for you to help me get what I want. I have been using decoys to wear you down or to keep your attention diverted and my hope is that you are going to give in.

Check requirement: I got what I wanted from the interaction. You may not be happy about it, but you are resigned to it and I consider that acceptable. I employed this approach and I got what I wanted, so now I have solid evidence that this approach works. This helps me justify using it again in the future. It builds my confidence and skill in using it. The results have fortified my position above you. Going North has strengthened my resolve that I can use my partner's resources to get what I want.

Going South

Now let's see what going South looks like:

Interaction Road Map™

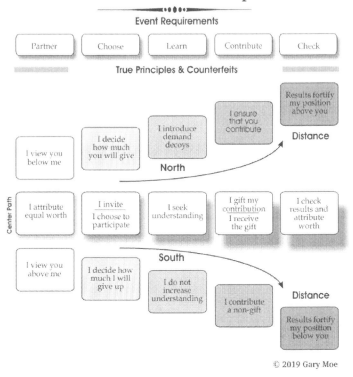

© 2019 Gary Moe

Partner: I view you above me

Choose: I decide how much I will give up

Learn: I do not increase understanding

Contribute: I contribute a non-gift

Check: Results fortify my position below you

This approach also may sound harsh just as it did when we were going North, however it is surprising how subtle this approach can be and how often it is employed. Let's look at it in more detail.

Going South is the typical response to a partner who has decided to go North.

Partner requirement: I view you above me. You are better than me either because you have convinced me it is so or I have concluded it for whatever reason.

Choose requirement: I have relinquished my right to choose and allow you or circumstance to do that for me. I have concluded that I have no choice, so I am already thinking about what this interaction is going to cost me. I am trying to decide how much I will have to give up before this is over.

You will hear people who have gone South saying such things as "I have to," "I must," "I can't," "I have no choice," etc.

Learn requirement: The demand decoys work well on me. I am lured away very effectively. If you say that I should feel guilty, I do. If you say that I am to blame, I believe you. If you bring up history to show that I am at fault, I have no way to counter it. I accept it. Even if I argue these things, it doesn't seem to make any difference. The requirement is to increase understanding, but I cannot seem to make any progress.

Contribute requirement: I give in and allow you to take what you want. This is not a gift. This thing you want still does not line up with what I want, but I will allow you to have it. Nothing about what has transpired thus far in the interaction makes me feel good. Viewing you as better than me, trying to decide how much I am going to have to give up, and being sucked in by decoys have not produced a single positive feeling thus far. The ordeal has been stressful and uncomfortable, so I have concluded that allowing you to have what you want is the way to bring relief from these other things. My hope is that getting to the end of this interaction will allow us to get back to some form of a normal relationship.

I may even believe that giving in is the more noble act since it appears that I am being the peacemaker, but I do not understand why I don't feel good about it.

Check requirement: The interaction is over. I don't feel good about it and this becomes just one more example that fortifies my position below you. I might view the feeling of relief that the interaction is over as a positive which is confusing. How can I feel relief when things are not good? The whole ordeal just strengthens my view that I am less.

Observations

The reason a person will go South when the other goes North is an attempt to maintain harmony in the relationship.

The problem is that going South eventually produces feelings of being used, of not being listened to, of being a second-class citizen, of being the person that seems to always be giving while the other seems to always be taking, and so forth. Sometimes that person who has been going South will try to break the cycle by going North. Unfortunately, both partners going North is another way to describe a fight.

The South partner goes North to break the cycle. The North partner will then go further North to re-establish a North/South positioning. The South partner will go further North and the cycle continues. This is the process of escalation using North strategies. This is a description of *a fight* using Center Path terminology. Once a fight begins then it is a matter of attrition to see who can last longer or go further North than the other with a focus on winning. The fight causes such disruption and chaos in the relationship that usually the person who typically goes South will return to going South to end the fight restore some semblance of harmony.

This attempt to break the cycle now becomes one more decoy that the North-going partner can use. It will essentially come out like this, "You see, if you would just stay South like you are supposed to, then we would not have these fights." The decoy is that the fight is the fault of the South-going partner.

Understanding these things, I can now expose one of the greatest relationship counterfeits. Remember the

Principle of Unity? The first law of that principle is: *The ultimate goal of a relationship is to produce unity between the relationship partners.*

I can now introduce the fifth law of the **Principle of Unity**: *The counterfeit of Unity is Harmony. Harmony is managed distance.*

Harmony in music sounds beautiful. In a relationship it is often perceived as a relief from more challenging things, so it is often misinterpreted as being the correct goal. Striving for harmony in a North/South relationship appears to be the best plan to keep the peace by keeping disruption and chaos to a minimum.

The interesting thing is that those who strive for harmony still feel that the relationship is unproductive and that it is not producing the expected level of happiness, fulfillment, and personal satisfaction. For people who typically goes South, the feelings of being used and neglected will be so confusing in the light of having achieved harmony. After all, they felt they were doing the more noble thing and that they were being the peacemakers.

Earlier I explained that a fight is when both partners go North. The silent treatment ensues when both go South because both partners are refusing to interact with each other. The goal of both approaches is to see who will cave in first, meaning who wins and who loses.

A relationship is not a competition, it's a partnership. A relationship never wins when partners go North and South.

The funny thing is that we all have a tendency to go North or South in certain circumstances. I will ask people, "If you are not going Center Path, do you tend to go North or South?" It is interesting to hear their responses.

Personally, my tendency is to go North so I watch for indications that I might have gone there unaware. The most telling of those indicators is how I am viewing my relationship partner in any given moment. I have found this to be the fastest and most efficient way to tell if I have gone North or South.

The other interesting tendency that people have is to go one way in one circumstance and the other in another. For example, some will admit they go North at work and South at home. Others will do the opposite. Our choice is driven by what we feel comfortable doing and what we believe will work.

Some years ago, I was working with a woman who was struggling in her work relationships. We had come to this point in our discussion of Center Path. I was explaining North and South, how sometimes the partners will switch positions to try and break the cycle, and then how they will switch back to regain harmony. I could tell that the concept was really resonating with her. Then I started to explain Center Path. I was only moments into it when I could see that she was visibly shaken by the idea. Then she said, "Oh my goodness, this is huge! There is a third option. I never knew that. There is a third option." From that point forward she was a sponge soaking up every detail. We talked for several hours reviewing unproductive interactions she had experienced and then reliving what they could have been using Center Path. When we were finished, she wanted to leave in a rush saying, "I have to go tell my daughter. This is huge."

Read through the following examples and see if you can tell if the relationship partners are going Center Path, North, or South. If you decide they are going North or South, identify who is doing what and why. If demand decoys are being used, identify them.

Example 1: Dave was nervous as he waited for his wife to get back from the store. He knew what he wanted to do, he knew what he had to do, but it was still nerve-wracking. When Karen got home, he was waiting with pictures from their last vacation. He sat her down and started showing the pictures being sure to point out the ones on the beach and mentioned several times in passing that he was so pleased that they had been able to do the things that she had wanted during the vacation. Then he said, "I really need to get some larger tires for my truck." She asked how much they would be and how he thought they could pay for them. He told her the price and suggested that some of it would need to come from their savings. Dave was sure that she would not like that idea and sure enough she did not. Dave pointed out that he had been willing to do the stuff she had wanted to on the vacation, now he was asking for similar consideration.

Example 2: Chris' 14-year-old daughter, Sara, has announced that she wants to go to a party with her friends this weekend and it will probably go until 3:00 a.m. the following morning. Chris told her that she could go, but she had to be home by midnight. Since that conversation Sara has been banging around the house, made her little brother cry twice, has not been gentle about closing doors, and has been doing her chores with such drama it was almost comical.

Example 3: Ben's mom has asked him several times today to get his chores done. The most recent time she asked, Ben was definitely frustrated. In a rather bold way for a 7-year-old, he asked why he had to do chores. Ben's mom was in the middle of three other things and impatiently said, "Because I am the mom and I said so."

Example 4: Leslie, Jake's mom, was sitting in the kitchen when Jake happened to walk by. She said, loud enough for him to hear, "A dutiful son would have taken the garbage out by now."

Example 5: The other day I was in the grocery store and heard a mother say to her son, "If you love me you will...."

Example 6: After dinner, Bob sat back down in his chair and told his wife of forty-five years, "I don't do dishes," and laughed. Bob's wife replied, "Yeah, I know," and started running the hot water in the sink.

Example 7: Sue did not like what her manager decided regarding the project. She felt that it just was not fair. At lunch, she brought it up with her friend in the accounting department. By the middle of lunch her friend was admitting that she was in full agreement with Sue's assessment. Sue felt good to be heard and to get empathy. Sue knew that she would see another of her friends at break and planned on telling her about the entire incident.

Notes

CHAPTER VII

Center Path

I have talked about the five events of an interaction, what a Center Path response looks like, and what going North and South looks like for each event.

Guiding an interaction to a productive outcome is so important to building relationship strength, delivering the repairing qualities of the principles, and improving the relationship overall that it is critical you are very good at going Center Path.

I want to take you on a deeper dive into how to formulate Center Path responses for each event, identify those things that will try to knock you off the path, and show you some of the traps you need to avoid.

Interaction Road Map™

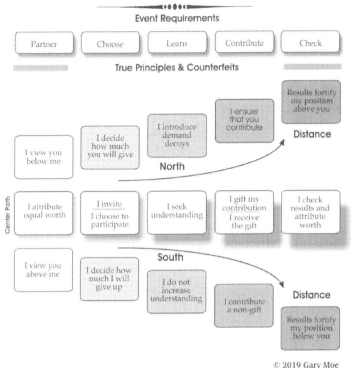

© 2019 Gary Moe

Partner: The requirement is to form the partnership. The Center Path response is to attribute equal worth, meaning *I attribute the same worth to you as I do myself.*

Attributing to you the same self-worth that I give myself has to happen independent of the hundreds of things that are different between us. This is the trap.

The amazing thing about this moment is that it transpires completely in my mind. It is all about perspective and it is made by choice.

The other amazing thing is that it cannot be faked. A person can try, but it will not work. People see through the façade almost immediately. I have watched individuals try to convince those around them that they were the recipients of equal worth and I have watched the recipients pretend they were convinced. It does not work. Everyone knows exactly where they stand, always.

So, how do I do it? How do I correctly participate in the first event when faced with all the differences between the two of us? How do I attribute the same worth to you when obviously I am smarter, or more experienced, or because I acted stupidly the last time we interacted, or you did, or I believe you owe me an apology, or I owe you one, or we just got done with a fight, or I don't like you, or you have caused me pain and it hurt, or I don't trust you, or I have caused you pain, or any one of hundreds of other things I could use to compare? How do I attribute the same worth to you as I do myself?

Everyone has to come up with their way of doing it. Personally, I look inside myself and sum up the worth I believe I have—no more, no less. I imagine myself gathering it altogether, like collecting it into a basket so that I can see how much I have. I gather it up and then I imagine my relationship partner holding the same basket with the same amount as I have — no more, no less.

Another way to do it is to picture your partner in front of you. Then imagine whether you are looking down at your partner, across at your partner, or up at your partner. Visualizing positions is very effective.

Everyone can figure out how to do it with a little practice and that is really what you need to do. Don't wait until you are in the interaction. You position before you start an interaction anyway, so practice outside the interaction until you have figured out your way. You will find an approach and imagery that works best for you. Whatever method or image you decide to use, you need to see, in your mind's eye, your partner standing in front of you with the same amount of worth as you have — no more, no less.

The epiphany comes when a person realizes that it is all about "my worth," not my partner's. The participation requirement has nothing to do with evaluating my partner's worth or value. It has everything to do with perception of my worth, no matter how much or how little I believe I have and then attributing to my partner a worth that is no more nor less than my own.

The moment a thought sneaks in to evaluate my partner's worth or value, instead of mine, then I know that North or South is trying to bully its way into the interaction. Evaluating anything other than my own worth is to go North or South.

I have mentioned this before, but it is such an important point that I need to mention it again. If a person gets this first step wrong, the interaction will begin to fall apart and *will* ultimately fail to produce the incremental increase in unity and positive feelings that it needs to produce.

It is impossible for the interaction to conclude otherwise. Getting it wrong means I have gone North or South. North and South are counterfeits. It is impossible for a counterfeit to produce good results. It just simply cannot happen. It is like squeezing an orange and expecting apple juice. The very thought of it sounds silly to us. Obviously, it is not possible. We know we cannot get apple juice out of an orange. In the same way, we need to understand that employing a counterfeit and expecting good results is just as silly and just as obviously not possible.

The reality is that counterfeits are pesky things. They hide in the shadows and try desperately not to become obvious. By their very nature, they are designed to create an illusion. Just think about counterfeit money. A counterfeiter never wants you to look at the money too closely. Instead he wants you to continue going about your daily routines. He wants your attention diverted someplace else so that the illusion can play out unimpeded. However, we are going to shine bright lights on these counterfeits to see them for what they really are, to see how they really behave, and to see what they really produce.

Let's move to the next event.

Choose: The want of the initiating partner is now presented. Along with this want, we discover there are three implied wants being placed on the table:

I want <u>you</u> as a partner

I want your <u>participation</u> in an interaction

I want your <u>response</u>

It now falls to the responding partner to choose a response to these three wants. If the responding partner decides that his response is "no," it could be because of any one of these three wants. For example, "I don't want to associate with you, therefore the rest of the things you want do not matter," "I don't mind associating with you and I don't mind participating in an interaction with you, but I can foresee that the want you are presenting is going to require more than I want to give or is not going to be beneficial to us or the relationship," and so forth.

Knowing about these three wants is useful for those struggling to have interactions with someone who is reluctant to interact or is openly resistant to it. The reluctance could have roots in a place you did not anticipate.

The second event has two slightly varied participation requirements. One is appropriate for the initiating partner and the other is for the responding partner. The requirement for the responding partner is to make a choice regarding the three wants we have been discussing.

The requirement for the initiating partner is to invite participation.

What does a Center Path invitation to participate look like?

The most common and well executed second event invitation is simply to say "please". Other ways that I have observed include a declaration that "it's going to be fun", "it won't take that long", "it's easy", it may come with an offer of help or an explanation of how to accomplish it, some people add humor, etc.

The thing that separates a Center Path invitation from going North is whether the initiating partner offends the **Principle of Choice**. A North approach will always offend the principle.

Let me demonstrate with a very simple example. John is in the living room and Kate is in the kitchen. Using this setting let's play out two scenarios:

Scenario 1--John: KATE, get in here!

Scenario 2--John: Kate, when you have a sec, can you please come here?

What is the difference between these two scenarios?

The difference is who makes the second event choice and who is supposed to make it.

John goes North in the first scenario. He wants Kate in the living room and concludes that the best way to make that happen is to alter the participation requirements to those of his own making. This allows him to introduce what he wants, make Kate's participation choice for her, and then announce both his want and her completed choice at the same time. He uses this approach in place of an invitation. John offends the **Principle of Choice** by his determination to make Kate's choice for her.

The second scenario is an invitation. John still has full expectation that Kate will come, but the difference is that John invites Kate and he ensures that Kate retains her choice. The **Principle of Choice** is not offended.

As I mentioned earlier--the thing to watch for is: Who is trying to make the second event choice?

If I am trying to make it for my partner, then I am going North. If I accept that my choice is being made for me, then I am going South.

When I invite and know that the choice resides with my partner, then I am going Center Path.

Let's move on to the third event.

Learn: The participation requirement is to learn. The response to that requirement is to seek understanding. Primarily the responsibility falls to the responding partner. The objective is to come to know, through the process of gathering more information, what the contribution needs to be to satisfy the want.

Let's use, as an example, a very simple interaction of one person asking another to pass the salt during a meal. After receiving the request to pass the salt, the requirement to learn may be little more than to scan the table to identify the location of the salt and assess whether it is within reach. Let's say that in the scan, the responding partner cannot see the saltshaker. The initiating partner, who is also under the requirement to help his partner gain understanding, knows where it is and so he educates his partner on where to find it. He fulfills his role by increasing the understanding of his partner.

During the third event, both partners are responsible for increasing understanding for each other and for themselves.

The Center Path response for both partners is simply to ensure that enough learning takes place between them for the interaction to complete successfully.

By contrast, if I am going North then I want to limit my partner's understanding to only those things I want him to know. Those things I want him to know do not necessarily have to be true. They are just facts that help me get what I want.

If I am going South, I am not interested in increasing understanding. My focus is on an exit plan and what is it going to cost me to get out of the interaction or to the conclusion of it.

Contribute: The Center Path response to contribute again varies slightly depending upon whether I am the initiating partner or the responding one. The responding partner gives his contribution to the initiating partner as he would give any other gift. The initiating partner must receive the contribution as he would a gift.

As the responding partner, I need to *give* my contribution as a gift. I deliberately use the word "give" instead of alternatives like "deliver," "drop off," "send," and so forth to make a specific point.

To give something means:

1. The act is not conditional — There are no terms, conditions, or expectations; I am not expecting anything in return
2. I have no ulterior motive — I have no hidden agenda or alternate reason for participating
3. There are no strings attached — The gift does not come with extra baggage, I am not trying to make a point or deliver some message

By contrast, if I were going North and were the initiating partner, my focus would be on extracting what I want from my partner. I do not view the contribution as a gift, but as an obligation that my partner owes me or as another available resource from which I can take things. I may describe it as a gift to help my partner feel better about giving it to me.

If I were the responding partner and had decided to go North, I would be making the contribution with conditions or expectations that I would be receiving something in return now or in the future. I would make the contribution with an agenda, to make a point, to deliver a message, I would do it with the expectation of being acknowledged or rewarded, etc.

If I were going South, I would feel like the contribution I was making was being extracted from me, it was not what I want, etc. I may feel that it was the price I needed to pay to return to or to maintain harmony in the relationship and to keep the peace. I may try telling myself that it was the noble thing to do, but I would not understand why that conclusion did not make me feel good about it.

Check: The requirement for this event is to check the results of the interaction.

All interactions produce an incremental increase in unity or distance. An interaction never leaves a relationship in the same place it was when it started. There will always be movement. The only question is direction.

An increase in unity may be experienced as an increase in trust or confidence in the relationship partner and his or her ability to participate productively in interactions. It could be experienced in the form of appreciation which engenders a desire to interact again. You may reflect on an interaction and enjoy thoughts or feelings of it having been a pleasant, fulfilling, or rewarding experience. If you come away from an interaction feeling that you would like to interact with the person again, you have just experienced an increase in unity.

However, if you come away from an interaction with less trust, little appreciation, or if the interaction made you feel uneasy, uncomfortable, unpleasant, reluctant, or if you feel that you will need to be more guarded next time, then you have just participated in an interaction that produced distance.

The Center Path response to checking results is to consciously look for the results, recognize that a portion of those results will be experienced as feelings, and accept them. Accepting them means that I acknowledge that they are the results I am getting today. If they are not that great, then at least they serve as information indicating my starting position and motivation to make improvements.

We have just been through each event in any given interaction. I have explained the Center Path response to each of these events and contrasted that response with the alternatives of going North or South.

It is time for a homework assignment. I strongly suggest you considering doing it. It is designed to help you become more aware of what is transpiring in relationship interactions.

Homework assignment:

1. As you interact with people, see if you can detect the moment they attribute worth. Give it some thought and come up with a way of describing how you attribute worth.

2. Make a note of how many times you go Center Path, North, and South in the first event. This is purely an observation exercise to increase awareness, so don't be critical of yourself.

3. See if you can start picking out the third event in interactions. This is the event of seeking understanding. Either observe your own interactions or see if you can identify the third event in the interactions of others.

4. Watch for how many times a contribution is given and received as a gift and how many times it is not. Observe your own interactions

or those of others.

5. See if you can detect increases in unity or distance produced by interactions. Watch for it in your own interactions or in those of others. When observing your own interactions, identify your resulting feelings.

6. Keep a journal. Note interesting things you observe and any insights you gain.

Notes

CHAPTER VIII

Responding with Center Path

In the previous chapter I explained how to formulate Center Path responses in an interaction and contrasted that with what it looks like to go North and South.

Now I want to show you how to apply Center Path responses when your relationship partner is going North or South. This is how you guide an interaction to a productive outcome.

What to Expect

The illusion of a North/South relationship is that both partners are getting what they want. North gets their wants satisfied and South gets harmony. However, the relationship is operating at the expense of unity and the other benefits available to a productive relationship.

The theme of going North is to change the rules of the interaction. North wants to control choices, exploit relationship resources, and compel the desired contribution. A person will employ a North approach because it has worked in the past and it seems like it will work again.

Typically, South is employed in response to a partner who has gone North. South is an attempt to maintain harmony. Harmony minimizes the conflict and helps avoid the disruption, chaos, and potential fights that would otherwise ensue. Remember that harmony means managing the distance that already exists between the partners. The objective is to not let the distance grow too great, but to manage it within acceptable levels.

Those who go South find themselves in a very confusing situation. South appears to be the way of the peacemaker, the more noble path, but those who go South are confused by the fact that the approach does not produce the expected positive and rewarding feelings. Those going South expect that their actions will produce increases of trust, closeness, greater levels of gratitude, and so forth, but do not.

Going North is only successful when the other partner goes South. When the South partner tries going Center Path, the North partner is going to sense this change and is likely to apply pressure to get the relationship back to North and South. The North partner is going to use the same strategies used to create the North/South relationship originally and the same strategies that have been employed all along to maintain

North and South. These strategies are North's responses to each event. (See the **Interaction Road Map™**). They are very efficient at getting a person to go South.

The use of demand decoys is designed to distract, disrupt, or cause chaos in the relationship. The objective is to make things unpleasant, awkward, or uncomfortable so that going South appears more attractive.

Using decoys puts such a strain on the relationship that the partner who usually goes South resigns and returns to going South. The North partner fortifies his win and feels vindicated. The North partner can lay the blame of the disruption at the feet of the South partner who usually concedes and assumes responsibility. This fortifies the trap of the North/South relationship.

Center Path with a Partner Who Goes North

Let's talk first about how to go Center Path with a relationship partner who is going North.

The tool needed is the **Interaction Road Map™**.

Interaction Road Map™

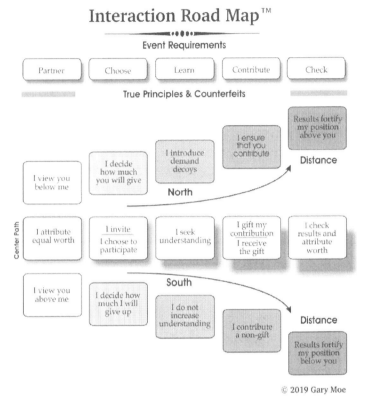

© 2019 Gary Moe

The first thing to understand is that a North partner is very practiced in using North strategies. This is how he or she keeps a South partner in check. Going Center Path is going to trigger the use of these strategies, but Center Path has a response for each of them.

If your relationship partner is open to talking about making improvements in your relationship, then that is a good place to start. If not, it does not mean that there is no hope. You actually have much you can do. The most powerful thing is to start going Center Path.

The second thing to understand is that your objective in going Center Path is simply that—to use Center Path responses. Do not try to get your partner to go Center Path. Do not be critical of your partner. Do not point things out such as showing what he or she is doing wrong, showing what things you are doing right, etc. Simply go Center Path. Respond with Center Path responses. Applying the principles correctly is powerful enough to bring about improvement in your relationship even if your partner is initially unaware, unwilling, or fully opposed to going there himself or herself.

Let's look at each interaction event. I will present the participation requirement and then discuss it.

Partner: My partner has gone North which means that he has positioned himself or herself above me. The Center Path response is that I attribute the same worth to my partner as I do myself.

It is easy to get caught in the trap of responding with emotion now that I know my partner considers himself or herself to be superior to me.

It is vitally important that I attribute worth correctly. Attributing worth needs to be practiced ahead of time. It cannot be faked or done randomly or haphazardly. I need to be confident I can do it correctly each time it is requircd.

I have seen how powerful this first response is in the face of a North-going partner. It sets the stage for every response I give from this point forward. This is the first step in breaking the cycle. It completely changes the landscape of the interaction and will, with continued use, change the relationship.

Choose: The Center Path response is that I choose.

North wants me to believe that my choice has already been made for me. The Center Path response is to remember that I retain my choice. I choose if I will participate and I choose how. If I choose to participate, then I choose to use Center Path.

Retaining my choice means that I protect choice for myself and for my partner. This is a protection of the **Principle of Choice**.

Let's go back to the example of John and Kate. Last time we looked in on them we watched two scenarios play out, one in which John goes North and the other in which he goes Center Path. Let's just look at the scenario when John goes North.

John is in the living room and Kate is in the kitchen. Using this setting let's play two scenarios:

John: KATE, get in here!

John wants Kate in the other room and has concluded that the best way to make that happen is to go North. He does so by altering the participation requirements from what a normal interaction requires to his script using a new set of requirements. These new requirements allow him to introduce the want, make Kate's participation choice for her, and then announce both the want and the completed choice at the same time. John sees event two as the moment to let Kate know that he has made her choice for her.

This scenario violates the **Principle of Choice**.

The irony of John's approach is that he can never take Kate's choice away from her. He can only try to make her think he has. He does this by switching the choice with another one. The new choice is: "I have already made your choice to participate in the interaction and now I am pressing you to accept the fact that I have done it." Unfortunately, if she accepts this new choice, she has gone South. The illusion is that it looks like she is choosing to participate, but that is not the choice she is making. Instead she is agreeing with the changes John is making including a switch in choices and she accepts the loss of her participation choice. She pays this price to buy harmony.

How does Kate respond to John using Center Path? Let's step through the events:

Kate wants to respond using Center Path. She accepts the fact that John is being a bit of a jerk right now. She consciously avoids positioning herself above him or below him. Instead she sees him with as much worth as she has. She pictures interacting with him on the same plane as she is.

She says to herself, "I choose to participate. I will go see what he wants, and I will do it because I choose to." She calls out to John from the kitchen, "John, I am coming. I will be right there."

Almost instantly Kate arrives in the living room. "John, I came as quickly as I could. What do you want?"

Kate's actions appear, to the outside observer, to be the same as if she had gone South, but her approach to her actions is significantly different. She consciously made the partnership assessment and did not let herself be swayed North or South by John's behavior. She retained her right to choose and did not let John take it from her. After arriving she asked what he wanted. She was there to learn.

Now check Kate's responses thus far using the **Interaction Road Map™**. How is she doing?

After addressing whatever it was that John wanted, Kate returned to the kitchen to continue doing what she was doing prior to the interaction. Kate enters the interaction calm and leaves it calm. She could have easily been sucked into going North and having an argument about John's approach, or South, feeling used and valueless. She simply chose not to go there.

The choice starts with the assignment of worth. I cannot stress this enough. People who are successful in their relationships know how to function in the first event very effectively.

Attributing worth is vitally important, but it is easy to be swayed by an emotional response. After John's outburst, Kate could have thought to herself, "You jerk," or she could have thought, "What have I done wrong?" She may not be able to avoid the initial emotional response, but what will happen if she lets it drive her response to the first event? She will go North or South. This is why practicing the action of attributing worth is so important. It helps to neutralize the emotional response and replace it with the Center Path response.

Story: A few years ago, I was working with a husband and wife. They had both been divorced and were now married to each other. They were having a few rough patches and were describing some of them to me. Before long, the wife said something very telling. She expressed that she was frustrated because her husband would not argue with her. She explained that she had learned in her previous marriage to resolve issues with a head to head fight. She firmly believed this was a resolution technique and was very frustrated when her new husband would not engage. I asked the husband about it and he said, "I won't engage in a fight. Nothing gets resolved, so I won't do it."

I tell this story because it is a great example of someone using Center Path. He retained his choice and used it by stating that he would not engage in a fight.

Not long after my initial conversation with this couple, I talked with the wife again. She said that she was making progress and trying very hard to find calm ways to resolve problems. She said that she felt it was working and that their relationship seemed better for it.

Let's move on to the next event.

Learn. At this point my North partner is going to sense that things are different in this interaction. He or she may likely conclude this as a threat to his or her position. He or she may be a bit confused as I am obviously not going South as I have typically done, but this time it's different because I am not going North either. My partner was expecting North if I was not going South, but the fight and the escalation is not materializing. This is when my partner will pull out the demand decoys and get to work.

The purpose of a demand decoy is to employ a strategy to establish or reestablish North/South positioning. Let's review my sample list of demand decoys. A North partner could use any of the following demand decoys or others I have not listed as part of this strategy.

These are some examples of demand decoys:

- Guilt
- History
- Baggage
- Emotions
- Pretend facts
- Anger
- Blame
- Changing the subject
- Proving a point
- Comparisons
- Positional power
- Silence
- Withholding
- Holding the relationship hostage
- Being the martyr
- Excuses
- Tantrums
- Keeping score
- Blackmail
- Rewards
- Punishment

A decoy is an illusion that attempts to take my attention away from one thing and place it on another. A North partner will use demand decoys to focus attention on North/South positioning in an effort to get what he or she wants.

Let's go back to John and Kate.

John: KATE, get in here!

John has gone North.

Kate retained her choice, came quickly, and said, "John, I came as fast as I could, what do you want?"

John: You never come when I tell you to. You always keep me waiting like I am not important.

John is not getting what he had hoped for. If Kate had responded with emotion, North or South, that would have been fine because John could keep the upper hand. He could maintain his position of being better than Kate. Instead, Kate has responded with courtesy. She attributed worth correctly, she chose to believe his request was urgent, and she came quickly. She has retained her choice.

What does John do? He throws out a demand decoy. How likely is it that he called her with such urgency just so he could tell her that she never responds with urgency? He has deployed a decoy.

What decoys did John use?

Looking at the list, I can see match ups with at least guilt, blame, keeping score, and comparisons. There may be more, but this is good enough for this example.

How does Kate respond and remain Center Path? The way she does it is by recognizing the decoys and refusing to get sucked in by them. She stays focused on Center Path responses.

Kate may say: It sounded like there was something urgent, how can I help you?

In this response, Kate is calmly ignoring the decoy and staying focused on the needs of the interaction.

This will hopefully get John back on the topic of whatever it was that he needed.

However, for this exercise, let's have John stay North and keep going North. To do so, John switches tactics and says that the urgent thing he needed was to discuss why she always keeps him waiting. By sticking with that story, he has tried re-positioning himself above Kate.

If Kate calls his bluff and says that was not the reason he called her, John can argue that indeed it was, and he has now set the stage for an argument which is not a problem at all for John since it would mean that he had Kate fully engaged in the decoy of a fight. If Kate ignores it and walks away, she has gone South and that reestablishes the North/South relationship, which again, is not a problem for John.

Kate needs a third option. Center Path is that option. It is typically the option not seen.

Center Path for Kate would be to ensure she continues attributing equal worth and retaining her choice. Doing so produces a response that could be something like this:

John, if that is what you want to talk about, then it must be important to you. If it is important to you, then it is important to me as well. I am happy to talk to you about it. I estimate that we will need about an hour to discuss it properly. I have things cooking on the stove and cannot leave them unattended that long so we can have this discussion later this evening or I can turn everything off and postpone dinner for a couple of hours and we can discuss it now. What would you like to do?

Let's take a look at Kate's response. She does not disagree or argue what John is thinking or feeling. This is always the proper position to take. No one can ever prove they know what another person is thinking or feeling. Instead, Kate continues to attribute equal worth. That allowed her to sincerely conclude: "If that is on your mind and important to you, then it is important to me." At this point, it does not matter if John wants to pursue this topic or return to whatever it was that triggered the interaction initially. Kate has shown that if it is important to John it is important to her. That position defuses all kinds of things.

All Kate has done so far is simply apply the principle correctly: I attribute the same worth to you as I do myself. Note that because of attributed equal worth, Kate can offer this conclusion, "If it is important to you, it is important to me." She can offer it with complete sincerity which means there is no hidden agenda, no ulterior motive, no baggage, no conditions, etc. She does not have to strategize, to guard herself, to concoct anything, to position herself, etc. It does not invoke

124

emotions of being tense, anxious, or fearful. This is a simple, straight forward response.

Next, Kate retains her freedom to choose and she exercises that freedom. She states that she chooses to have a discussion with John, she shows that she is a willing participant in deciding when that discussion can take place, and she shows that she chooses to willingly invest personal resources in having it. Not only does she retain her freedom to choose, but she also protects his freedom to choose by giving him choices and asking him to choose as well.

Finally, Kate shows that she is sincere and is ready to take the matter seriously if John feels the same way. She estimates that it will take an hour to discuss properly and offers to postpone dinner to do it. Both of these suggestions show that she is willing to invest her personal resources toward addressing the matter and is inviting John to do the same. The beauty of this approach is that it puts the onus back on John. He either has to declare that the decoy is important, or he has to drop it. If John declares it as important, then Kate and John will discuss it and hopefully resolve it. This does two things:

1. It removes the issue from becoming a decoy in the future.
2. It shows John how Kate is willing to address any other decoys he may decide to use in the future.

Let me say this again. All Kate did was continue to attribute equal worth and retain freedom of choice for herself and her partner. She did that in part by giving her partner choices and inviting him to choose.

I realize in this example that John is being a jerk. That makes this example a good one because the natural tendency of most people is to respond with emotion or by being a jerk back. Unfortunately, all that does is perpetuates the same kinds of unproductive interactions that a relationship has probably already been experiencing. It is a vicious cycle. It will not stop until someone steps outside the cycle and breaks it.

I also realize that it is not easy to try to keep emotions under control while trying to come up with a Center Path response. In fact, it is not unusual to look at Kate's response in this example and conclude that, "I could never come up with a response like that." It may seem like that at first but let me contrast that feeling with this observation: All Kate did was continue attributing equal worth and she protected choice by creating choices and inviting both herself and John to choose.

These two things are not hard. They just take a little bit of practice. In fact, if you find yourself in an interaction with a North-going partner, each time you need to respond in the interaction, just ask yourself, "What response can I give that attributes worth and protects choice?"

Kate's response was only one of a number of responses she could have made. As long as she honored the principles of attributing worth and protecting choice, any response she chose would have been both right and effective.

Now comes the marvelous part. If you combine what you know about your partner's personality and character with the principles of attributing worth and protecting choice, not only will you come up with a correct response, but that response has the potential of being highly customized and specifically designed for your partner. In these situations, the response can be highly impactful.

Contribute: The Center Path response is that I view giving and receiving the contribution as a gift.

This may sound like an odd requirement, but it is powerful once you know what is transpiring. When a partner goes North, it is abusive to the relationship. Giving a contribution as a gift brings an element of nobility to the relationship to counteract the abuse. It does not matter if I am the initiating or the responding partner, if I treat my contribution as a gift, it will have a positive impact on the interaction and the relationship.

The amazing thing is that it only takes the choice to treat the contribution as a gift for it to have a positive impact on the interaction and the relationship.

Check: The Center Path response is that I check results and attribute worth.

I check the results of the interaction. One facet of the results will be the way I feel. In the example of John and Kate, it appears that Kate was able to return to the kitchen feeling calm.

Some people may express feelings of winning. This can be good in one circumstance and not so good in another. If the person feels like the win was beating their partner, then they have gone North. That is what "attributing worth" addresses. Beating a partner positions that person below the other.

However, if the feeling of winning is associated to a win for the relationship, then that is good. It was a win for the relationship. The relationship has just experienced a Center Path interaction. Results may not yet be as good as they could be, but they are at least headed in the right direction.

Attributing worth in the fifth event is the same as attributing it in the first one.

Summary

The theme of going North is to position relationship partners unevenly, control choices, exploit relationship resources, and compel the desired contribution. Center Path responses to North initiatives neutralize every strategy, and it does so from a position of neutrality which is void of criticism, judgement, or attack.

Center Path with a Partner Who Goes South

We have been reviewing how to respond to a partner who is going North. South usually is the response, but Center Path offers a third option.

Going South is often the chosen option when the other partner goes North. This is a reactive response to try and maintain harmony. However, there are times when a person proactively chooses to go South, not because of a reaction to a partner going North, but simply because South is their strategy.

There are a variety of characteristics associated with going South. Some of them include:

- Feeling reluctant to participate in an interaction
- Walking away from an interaction part way through
- Contributing minimally
- Appearing shy
- Not appearing comfortable interacting
- Only engaging in an interaction if it interests them
- Preferring non-personal interactions via texting and social media
- Expressing fear and anxiety when engaging with people, especially those they do not know

Common reasons a person will choose South in response to Center Path include low trust, low self-esteem, conditioned response from being in other North/South relationships, learned response from observing others, minimal positive experiences from interactions, a belief that they can avoid of being judged, etc.

Going South means minimal contributions in interactions. I would suggest assessing the relationship maturity. You may need to strengthen the relationship using the **Relationship Strengthening Methodology**.

If these efforts do not help, then there are a few more things that you need to know so that your efforts will have more influence.

These things are found in the book entitled "*The Nurturing Relationship*." You will need to engage your partner in a Nurturing Relationship to help them interact more productively.

Notes

CHAPTER IX

The Relationship Landscape

Let's review the **Principles of Relationships**, the **Relationship Maturity Model™**, the **Relationship Strengthening Methodology**, the Interaction Participation Requirements, and what it means to go Center Path, North, and South.

The Governing Principles of Relationships

1) **Principle of Choice**
   I.   *Both relationship partners have the freedom to choose*

2) **Principle of Interactions**
   I.   *Interactions are the building blocks of all relationships*
   II. *An interaction is composed of five events. These events transpire the same way every time, everywhere, for everyone.*
   III. *Each event has a participation requirement. How a person responds to the participation*

requirements determines how productive or unproductive the interaction will be.

IV. There are only three possible responses to each participation requirement. One response is correct and will produce good results. The other two responses are counterfeits and can only produce poor results.

3) Principle of Relationship Maturity

I. Relationship maturity is observable and can be measured by the level of contribution both partners are willing to make.

II. There are seven levels of maturity that a relationship may achieve. Each level is characterized by a type of contribution.

III. A relationship develops by progressing through the levels of maturity until arriving at the level appropriate for that type of relationship

IV. Any attempt or expectation to get your partner to skip a contribution level will produce disruption in the relationship, distrust, and distance between the partners

V. The only way to invite a relationship partner to contribute at a higher level is to contribute there first. This creates the perfect invitation without violating any principles.

VI. Both partners must be willingly contributing at a given maturity level before the relationship can declare that it is functioning at that level.

4) Principle of Unity

I. Successful relationships naturally produce unity between the relationship partners.

II. Capacity for greater unity increases with relationship maturity.

III. The opposite of unity is distance.

IV. An interaction will always produce an incremental increase in unity or distance.

V. The counterfeit of Unity is Harmony. Harmony is managed distance.

Relationship Maturity Model™

7 – Selfless Service
6 – Commitment
5 – Partnership Resources
4 – Personal Resources
3 – Meaningful Information
2 – Courtesy
1 – Acknowledgement

Strengthening Methodology

1. Identify the level at which your relationship partner is willing to contribute.

2. Initiate a series of interactions where the only objective is to make that level's required contribution. Continue initiating these interactions until the relationship stabilizes. Be patient. Sometimes this make take a while depending upon how beat up the trust is.

3. When the relationship has stabilized, invite your relationship partner to the next level of maturity. The only way this can be done is by going there

first and making the appropriate contribution.

4. Continue initiating interactions with this objective until your relationship partner responds with the same level of contribution. Then go back to step one and start again.

Interaction Road Map™

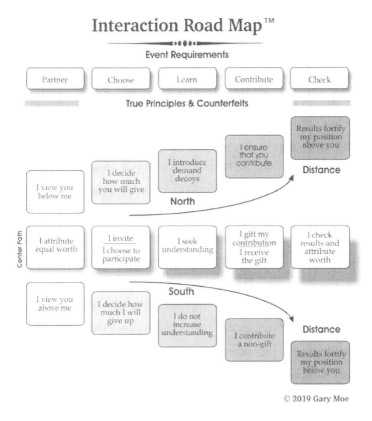

© 2019 Gary Moe

CHAPTER X

Summary

My hope is that you see relationships with a new perspective. You now have the governing principles and the tools you need to initiate, maintain, and improve a relationship.

We have talked about how the interaction is the heart of a relationship. Productive interactions are the means by which you can build relationship strength and by the repairing qualities of the principles can be delivered to a relationship.

You now know how to guide an interaction to a productive outcome by going Center Path.

Take the time to do the homework assignments. Keep a journal, even if it is brief. Note your insights as they happen and then go back and review them from time to time.

Productive relationships are within your reach. Pursuing them is worth the time and effort required. They are the greatest source of long-term, sustainable happiness.

CHAPTER XI

Next Steps

This book has focused on the Principles of Relationships. The second book in the True Principles Series is called "*Natural Prosperity*." In it I describe what it means to meet the demands of reality. I present the governing principles and show how to apply them.

These two books form the core of what a person needs to know for personal success.

The two most common reasons for exploring Center Path are: 1) A person wants to achieve greater success in his or her personal life, and 2) A person is in a relationship with someone who needs help achieving greater success in his or her life. Examples include a spouse wanting to help a spouse, a parent wanting to help a child, an employer wanting to help an employee, a teacher wanting to help a student, etc.

"*The Nurturing Relationship*" is the third book in the True Principles Series. It builds on the core principles found in the first two books and shows how to effectively help a relationship partner be more successful.

Beyond these three books, there will be a set of application books designed to help people apply the principles in targeted relationships. The purpose of these books is to demonstrate a tightly focused application of the principles in specific circumstances. My experience has shown that people generally grasp the core principles quite easily, but they more examples of how to apply the principles in their specific circumstances. The application books are designed to assist in that area.

More information about the books can be found at: www.TruePrinciples.com

On the website you will also find a growing number of articles, more specific examples, class offerings, and other services as they become available. Announcements about new material and additional offerings can be found at the site, as well.

Acknowledgements

To my wife I express my most profound love, gratitude, and appreciation for standing by my side through thick and thin. You are my best friend, the love of my life, and the safe harbor in the storm. You make everything enjoyable. Thank you for being my companion in this journey through life.

To each of our wonderful children I thank you for your constant love and kindnesses. Each of you mean the world to me and I am grateful to call you my own.

Additional Publications by Gary Moe

Natural Prosperity: Compliments *Center Path Relationships* by describing how to successfully meet the demands of reality.

These two books form the core of what a person needs to know to be substantially more successful in life.

The Nurturing Relationship: Describes how to help their relationship partner who may be having their own struggles being successful in relationships and/or meeting the demands of reality.

More information about these and other publications can be found at: www.TruePrinciples.com

About the Author

Gary is the son of a WWII veteran, the grandson of a WWI veteran, and the product of a kind and caring mother. His father was a surveyor who, for forty-two years, helped map the western United States, Hawaii, Saipan, and American Samoa. His father's career created a unique environment in which to grow up as Gary moved with his family forty times before he was nineteen. He quickly learned the value of relationships with family and friends.

Gary earned a degree in Anthropology and studied nine languages to compliment his fascination with relationships, cultures, and the nature of human character.

Drawing on a broad range of life experiences and observations, Gary became intrigued with the question: *What causes some relationships to be productive and others to be unproductive and strained?*

He has discovered some interesting answers to his question. He is now eager to share what he has learned with those who are searching for ways to improve and enjoy their own relationships.

Gary and his wife Nicole have seven children and seven grandchildren which keep their lives running at full speed.

Disclaimer

The information provided in this book is designed to provide helpful information and motivation on the subjects discussed. This book is not meant to be used, nor should it be used, to diagnose or treat any medical condition. For diagnosis or treatment of any medical problems, consult your own physician. The author is not responsible for any specific health needs that may require medical supervision and is not liable for any damages or negative consequences from any treatment, action, application or preparation, to any person reading or following the information in this book. This book is sold with the understanding that the author is not engaged to render any type of psychological, legal, or any other kind of professional advice. The content of this book is the sole expression and opinion of its author.

While best efforts have been used in preparing this book, the author makes no representations or warranties of any kind and assume no liabilities of any kind with respect to the accuracy or completeness of the contents and specifically disclaim any implied warranties of merchantability or fitness of use for a particular purpose. The author shall not be held liable or responsible to any person or entity with respect to any loss or incidental or consequential damages caused, or alleged to have been caused, directly or indirectly, by the information or programs contained herein. No warranty may be created or extended by sales representatives or written sales materials.

The author shall not be liable for any physical, psychological, emotional, financial, or commercial damages, including, but not limited to, special, incidental, consequential or other damages. You are responsible for your own choices, actions, and results.

Made in the USA
Lexington, KY
24 October 2019